The Arthur Negus Guide to English
POTTERY AND PORCELAIN

BERNARD PRICE

Foreword by Arthur Negus

Consultant Editor: Arthur Negus

Hamlyn

London · New York · Sydney · Toronto

Frontispiece: White Stoneware 'Minster' jug, *c.* 1840. Victoria and Albert Museum, London.

Published by
The Hamlyn Publishing Group Limited
London · New York · Sydney · Toronto
Astronaut House
Feltham, Middlesex
England

© Copyright
Bernard Price 1978

ISBN 0 600 37165 4

Filmset in England by
Photocomp Limited, Birmingham
Printed in England by
Hazell Watson & Viney Limited,
Aylesbury, Bucks

Contents

Acknowledgements

The author and publishers are particularly grateful to Mr Geoffrey Godden for allowing the following illustrations which are of items in the Godden Reference Collection to be included in this book: 13, 14, 18, 20, 21, 26, 28, 99, 100, 101, 103, 104, 105, 106, 107, 109, 111, 112, 113, 114, 115, 116, 117, 118, 119, 120, 124, 126, 128, 131, 136, 138, 141, 144, 145.

Illustration numbers 17, 31, 36 and 69 are reproduced by courtesy of the Birmingham Museums and Art Gallery and number 129 by courtesy of the Trustees of the Dyson Perrins Museum, Worcester.

Photographs
Ashmolean Museum, Oxford 16; Birmingham Museums and Art Gallery 17, 31, 36, 69; British Museum, London 8, 12, 30, 41, 44, 50, 60; City Museum and Art Gallery, Stoke-on-Trent 58; Dyson Perrins Museum, Worcester 129; G. W. Elliott, Stoke-on-Trent 5, 32, 33, 46, 53, 54; Fitzwilliam Museum, Cambridge 22, 65, 73, 108; Hamlyn Group–Walter Gardiner Photography 13, 14, 18, 20, 21, 26, 28, 99, 100, 101, 103, 104, 105, 106, 107, 109, 111, 112, 113, 114, 115, 116, 117, 118, 119, 120, 124, 126, 128, 131, 136, 138, 141, 144, 145; Hamlyn Group Picture Library 2, 3, 4, 19, 24, 25, 27, 29, 35, 45, 51, 61, 62, 63, 64, 66, 67, 77, 78, 89, 90, 91, 92, 121, 122, 123, 125, 130, 132, 133, 134, 135, 139, 140, 143; Merseyside County Museums, Liverpool 23, 75, 76; Museum of London 10, 11; Nottingham Castle Museum 68, 70; Royal Scottish Museum, Edinburgh 6, 34, 72; Royal Worcester Spode, Worcester 127; Victoria and Albert Museum, London 9, 15, 37, 38, 39, 40, 42, 43, 47, 48, 49, 52, 55, 56, 57, 59, 71, 74, 83, 97, 98, 102, 110, 142, 146; Josiah Wedgwood and Sons, Barlaston 1, 7, 79, 80, 81, 82, 84, 85, 86, 87, 88, 93, 94, 95, 96, 137.

Marks
The following marks are reproduced with the permission of the publishers W. Foulsham & Co. Ltd. from their Identification Guide, *English Pottery and Porcelain Marks* by S. W. Fisher:
1. Bow china works: Anchor and Dagger Mark, painted, *c.* 1760-76; mark in underglaze blue, *c.* 1760-76; early incised marks. 2. Bristol marks. 3. Chelsea-Derby marks. 4. Coalport Porcelain Works: mark in enamels or in gold, *c.* 1851-61; an early painted mark, *c.* 1805-15. 5. Longton Hall works. 6. New Hall porcelain works. 7. Plymouth porcelain works. 8. Minton. The Doulton and Martin ware marks are reproduced from *The Encyclopedia of British Pottery and Porcelain Marks* by Geoffrey Godden, Barrie and Jenkins, 1964; the Wedgwood marks from the catalogue of the Wedgwood Museum, Barlaston; the Royal Crown Derby marks from *The Story of Royal Crown Derby China* by John Twitchett FRSA. The remaining marks are all taken from *The Handbook of British Pottery and Porcelain Marks* by Geoffrey Godden, Herbert Jenkins Ltd., 1968.

The author and publishers would also like to thank Penguin Books Limited for permission to quote from *The Travels of Marco Polo* translated by R. E. Latham, 1958, © Ronald Latham 1958. The letters of Père d'Entrecolles are reproduced by kind permission of B. T. Batsford Limited, from *Burton's Porcelain, its Art and Manufacture*, published in 1906.

Finally, the author and publishers are grateful to The Hayward Art Group who did the line drawings.

Foreword by Arthur Negus

During the autumn of 1967 a BBC programme 'Talking about Antiques' appeared on the radio, and as a consequence, I first met Bernard Price. This programme has run each year ever since from September to the end of March, consequently over the past ten years I have met him regularly.

A true enthusiast, he is always ready to delve deeply into any subject that interests him and, in particular, into the area of his greatest interest – English Pottery and Porcelain. I feel this appreciation of his subject is apparent in what he writes and will appeal to you all when you read this, his first book on the subject.

I am well aware that there is now an apparently unending supply of new books on all subjects included within the all embracing term Antiques and the Fine Arts. But I do feel that Bernard Price's approach, concentrating on and dealing in detail with the different English factories will prove of especial interest and be of great value to collectors. He writes not just about the ideal, the perfect specimen firmly behind museum glass but of pieces that he has handled, with all their imperfections, and of a type which without too much difficulty, or expense, you too may handle and possess.

This personal approach, which will prove of great help to collectors is also adopted in this book's companion volume on English Furniture written by Robin Butler. Together they form the beginning of a new series of collector's reference books.

Arthur Negus

Chapter 1

An approach to collecting

It is only during the past thirty years that there has been widespread popular interest in antiques. In fact the demand for information concerning the objects made and used in the past appears now to be insatiable. A mystique once enveloped the subject entirely, giving the general impression that certain private individuals and the antique trade in general were apparently born with the requisite insight which the rest of us would find impossible to acquire. There is no doubt that knowledge was jealously guarded, in the belief that if the public knew too much professionals would find it more difficult to buy. Competition does undoubtedly still exist, but at the same time the market for antiques has expanded dramatically even on an international scale.

One reason for the expansion in demand is that it is now no longer only the enthusiasts, the connoisseurs and the true collectors who are interested in antiques and works of art, but also investors. In my experience the latter, not having a clear idea of what to collect, frequently buy on advice and consequently neither acquire good investments nor make good collectors. Yet what is meant by the term 'good collector'? In the second half of the twentieth century, the question of what to buy is one that is most frequently asked, although true collecting depends on instinct as much as on acquired knowledge, and no one person can really say exactly what, and what not, to collect. Yet with this warning in mind, I hope in the following pages to give you some idea of what collecting entails, the paths to follow and the pitfalls to avoid.

Value is always an important consideration for the collector, and the best advice to be given is to always buy the very best pieces you can afford. Do not pay high prices for damaged or heavily restored items unless they are exceptionally rare; always seek out objects in the best condition possible. Avoid the tendency of many people caught in the first flood of their new enthusiasm who frequently try to gather together a collection of their chosen interest overnight: it is far better to purchase one or two really fine pieces a year than fifty commonplace ones in a month. Always remember too that the value of a collection is by no means simply the sum of the prices of each individual object, but rather that each newly acquired item will enhance the value of its companions. Never pay more than you can really afford for any piece, for should you be forced to sell it again shortly afterwards, it is quite possible that you would lose money. Prudent buying depends not only on what you pay on purchase, but also on choosing the right time to sell.

Never collect indiscriminately. To be a magpie may be fun, but it may also be quite meaningless. When you have found an area of collecting that interests you, stay with it: study it carefully and attempt to make the subject your own, but above all enjoy it. Very few bargains are to be purchased today by a collector who is uninformed, but a thorough grasp of your own specialisation will often reveal the wise purchase and also show you what to reject. The collector with knowledge will always reap both pleasure and profit.

There are of course people who on the surface appear to need no advice on collecting. These can usually be recognised by such remarks as 'I don't know anything about it but I do know what I like, and I collect what I like.' This is all very well but if collectors do not understand what they are collecting then the objects they acquire and lovingly cherish may be no more than rubbish. Look long at the objects that interest you, and compare one with another, for it can be alarming to discover how often individual ideas of quality may vary.

Quality, value and interest should therefore be the key words of any collection. A major pitfall to the collector may be fashion. Popular band-wagons should always be avoided, and the publicity given to objects made by some particular modeller or manufacturer treated with scepticism.

The law of supply and demand will always apply and values are therefore created by the intensity of demand coupled with the supply of objects on the open market. Usually, by the time something has become fashionable, the real collections have already been made, and the latecomers pay high prices for what is left. On the other hand it is still possible, surprising though it may seem, to find areas of the applied arts which are relatively unexplored, or even ignored, by the collector, and these are always worth investigating. It takes no courage, only money, to return from an antique dealer or an auction room with a piece whose current value is high; it requires both courage and knowledge to purchase something for which there

9

appears to be little or no demand. You will need your courage for when you bring your purchase home, or show it to your friends, only to be met with raised eyebrows or even such comments as 'Whatever did you buy that for?'! Take heart, for this happens to all collectors.

It is surprising how rapidly attitudes change towards objects as their value begins to rise. In other words, money invariably brings respectability to items previously regarded as unworthy of serious consideration. A few illustrations will make this point clear. If an antique dealer or an auctioneer had called at your home ten years ago in order to prepare a valuation for insurance, he would undoubtedly have commented approvingly upon your country-made Welsh dresser, and with equal aplomb would have dismissed at a glance the Staffordshire blue-and-white transfer printed earthenware objects that might have been displayed upon its shelves. At that time such pottery could be bought for shillings, and it was this very fact that apparently blinded everyone to the interest and quality that much of it possessed. Yet once recognised, and documentation on it begun, the status of this humble earthenware rose dramatically and continues to do so.

A similar phenomenon can be seen in the rise over the last twenty-five years of the importance of the Victorian Staffordshire pottery portrait figure, originally made to brighten the mantelshelves of the cottager. In 1953, the first book devoted solely to these figures was published by a man named Brian Latham. Previously attention had been given almost entirely to the Staffordshire products of the eighteenth century. Mr

1 Part of a Wedgwood service decorated with the famous water-lily pattern. The decoration here is both painted and transfer printed. First made at Etruria in 1807, the service has been reproduced several times since, particularly in the form of blue-and-white transfer printed earthenware.

2 A pair of Victorian named portrait figures depicting the highwaymen Dick Turpin and Tom King, and with the names visible. Staffordshire.

Latham, however, was the first person to realise that the cheap popular Victorian portrait figure, decorated in very strong colours, offered a vast and highly picturesque panorama of Victorian history. These pieces, although lacking the elegant sophistication of earlier porcelain figures, represented a whole cavalcade of kings and queens, generals, sportsmen, actors and actresses, and even murderers and evangelists. When part of the Latham collection was sold in London the blinkers again fell away from the prejudiced eyes of many buyers, with the result that today not only are a number of lavishly illustrated books devoted to the subject but also some antique dealers now specialise in these wares. The reason why such pieces were overlooked for so long is that they were generally, and quite wrongly, compared unfavourably with earlier fine figure

3 White pottery swans shaped into plant holders were very popular in Victorian homes. The swan, sometimes regarded as a symbol of death, was used to contain evergreen plants, which in turn symbolised eternal life.

groups from English, or even Continental, porcelain factories. Yet such comparisons are invalid and the two products represent two different types of ceramic art destined for two different markets. Victorian Staffordshire portrait figures represent a popular folk art as vigorous as any to be found in the world. It is only in very recent years that we have begun to see the Victorian era in its true perspective, and its products are appreciated for themselves.

It is hoped that these two illustrations will serve as cautionary tales not to follow the prevailing fashion, but to pursue above all whatever captures your imagination. When an object interests you, then if it has quality and historical interest, handle it carefully, and bear the following points in mind. Above all, look for marks, but feel also the glaze and note carefully the colouring. Be aware of the weight: is it heavy for its size or is it surprisingly light? What does the object

4 Parian vase by Samuel Alcock & Co., Burslem, England, c. 1850. Victoria and Albert Museum, London.

5 Staffordshire slipware model of a cradle decorated in green and brown on a white slip ground. Late seventeenth or early eighteenth century. City Museum and Art Gallery, Stoke-on-Trent.

represent? Are there any emblems or other motifs to provide you with a clue? Is the mark under or over the glaze? Has the mark been impressed or stamped into the clay? Or has it been incised with a sharp object? (If impressed the mark will have been evenly applied with a stamp, if incised the line of the mark will have cut a furrow like a miniature plough.) All of these details may be of great importance when trying to establish the provenance or date of the object. It will also help if you have a good magnifying glass and a pocket reference book to help you identify marks that apply both to pottery and porcelain (you will find a suggested reading list at the end of this book).

Should you be able to find others with similar collecting interests there is much to be gained from discussing your collections and new purchases together. If you can make friends with an established collector then so much the better; it will also help to get on good terms with as many antique dealers as possible who specialise in the objects which interest you. Many collectors are suspicious of dealers, but they are in fact an essential part of the collecting process. You will find that most good antique dealers are usually prepared to discuss and exchange information with the genuine collector, and a long-term acquaintance with one will invariably prove fruitful. Once a dealer understands the type of collection you hope to form, or knows of its gaps, he can be of great help, for you will find that his network of contacts and coverage of auction sales will almost certainly be wider than your own. All collectors worth their salt will admit to having made mistakes and the new collector must be prepared to make some too.

Having considered the things which a new collector needs to be aware of when choosing objects and building his collection, I shall move on to the question of where to buy. This is an area where great caution must be exercised. There are, for example, many stallholders at the antiques markets which abound today, and it would seem rather foolish to pay a similar price at one of these to that which would be asked in a porcelain gallery in the West End of London. Yet all too often this is precisely what happens.

Markets have changed greatly in character in the last decade, with an influx of amateur dealers. Wherever you buy, in order to safeguard yourself, always obtain a receipt for the money you pay, together with the dealer's full description of the object that you have bought. Read it carefully, for it is this document that you will find essential under any claim you might lodge under the Misrepresentation Act. Until you have the confidence and expertise to buy elsewhere the best advice is to buy from established dealers.

In London many excellent specialist auction sales are held regularly throughout the year, and although attending them may bring pain as well as pleasure, there are few better places than the auction room in which to learn. The new collector may feel somewhat daunted by the suggestion that he should visit the famous London firms, as saleroom reports have now become a regular feature in several national newspapers and it is usually the more expensive objects that are mentioned and which claim the headlines. In fact most sales of pottery and porcelain cover an extremely wide field and you will be surprised at the number of pieces that sell for less than £100. Another difficulty is that many people are diffident about bidding at public auction sales. If you really cannot bring

6 *Far left:* Liverpool delft puzzle jug with pierced decoration (that is, decoration carried through the walls of the vessel typical of such jugs and painted in blue, *c.* 1750. These jugs were a 'joke' of the period as their contents could only be drunk by covering the side spouts in the rim and sucking the forward spout – the handle and rim being hollow! Royal Scottish Museum, Edinburgh.

7 *Above:* Wedgwood plate with design by Emile Lessor. The work of this French artist is highly distinctive, and he particularly favoured child groups. He worked at the Wedgwood factory between 1858 and 1863 and later continued to produce designs in France.

yourself to bid, then ask someone else to do it for you. The auctioneer's clerk will bid without charge on your behalf, and if you come to know the sales staff well you will certainly find someone ready to oblige. Many antique dealers unable to attend sales frequently make their presence felt by proxy bidding of this kind. If you watch carefully and follow the techniques used you will find the confidence to do it for yourself, and will experience considerable pleasure and satisfaction in the process.

Many of the larger London firms produce catalogues that have been made up with great care and scholarship. Most firms supply these catalogues at an annual subscription rate, and half a day armed with one at the viewing of a sale could not be better spent. You will become fully acquainted with the scope of the subject in which you are interested, and you will also be able to check your own identifications with those of the catalogue. For a fee they will also provide a printed list of the prices obtained following the auction, and again this will help to build up a sense of value and an awareness of what is scarce. Many provincial auctioneers now follow the same practice.

When you check the catalogue descriptions, also check carefully the object that you wish to buy for any tell-tale signs of restoration. It needs to be remembered that enormous advances have been made in restoration techniques in recent years, and such major work as the addition of new limbs to a pottery or porcelain figure may often be achieved in such a way as to be quite invisible to even the experienced eye. Restoration can always be revealed under ultra-violet light and most leading auctioneers and antique dealers are prepared to either guarantee an object as being free from restoration or to define the extent of it. Whenever possible, it is well worth while purchasing damaged objects very cheaply, for there is much to be learned from the examination of such pieces, as we shall discover in the following chapter.

Once you have been to a number of sales, you will come to appreciate more fully the particular fascination of pottery and porcelain. Part of this lies in the unique way in which its story is interwoven with that of man himself: it has existed since pre-historic times as part of human culture and when archaeologists want to find out more about a particular civilisation, it is fragments of its pottery that they seek above all else.

8 Leeds pottery figure of a girl, with an impressed mark on the base. Late eighteenth century. British Museum, London.

Although the terms pottery and porcelain may seem confusing to the new collector, the differences are quite straightforward. Pottery is a simple earthenware made from

15

ordinary clays that are widely obtainable. It is always opaque and needs glazing if it is to contain water. Porcelain, on the other hand, is the product of the much rarer china clay known as kaolin which, when fired, becomes translucent. It is on the whole much more impervious to water than pottery, but needs to be glazed at least on the inside if it is to be made into objects of everyday use such as teapots. Unglazed, it can be used for figure modelling.

The art of making porcelain is therefore much more complex, and was first discovered by the Chinese during the T'ang dynasty (618-906 AD). By the Middle Ages both Chinese pottery and porcelain was known throughout the Middle East and even in Africa. It was carried by sea and by hazardous journeys overland which followed ancient caravan routes. The first European to see porcelain was probably Marco Polo, the great merchant and explorer who travelled across Asia and into China as far as the court of the Great Khan in the late thirteenth century. There is a passage in his famous journal that particularly captures the excitement and adventure to be found in the study of ceramics:

'Let me tell you further that in this province, in a city called Tinju, they make bowls of porcelain, large and small, of incomparable beauty. They are made nowhere else except in this city, and from here they are exported all over the world. In the city itself they are so plentiful and cheap that for a Venetian groat you might buy three bowls of such beauty that nothing lovelier could be imagined. These dishes are made of a crumbly earth or clay which is dug as though from a mine and stacked in huge mounds and left for thirty or forty years exposed to wind, rain, and sun. By this time the earth is so refined that dishes made of it are of an azure tint with a very brilliant sheen. You must understand when a man makes a mound of this earth he does so for his children; the time of maturing is so long that he cannot hope to draw any profit from it himself or to put it to use, but the son who succeeds him will reap the fruit . . .'

The first appearance of porcelain in Europe resulted in attempts to manufacture it that were to continue until the eighteenth century, when the young German apothecary Johann Bottger made his first successful experiments at Meissen on the outskirts of Dresden. It was not until the middle of that century that porcelain was made on a wide scale in England.

Connoisseurs of pottery and porcelain, no matter what their field of specialisation, accept that the finest ceramic achievements in the world are those of the Chinese. The highest price yet achieved at auction by a ceramic object is £420,000, paid for a blue-and-white Ming bottle of the early fifteenth century, although half a million pounds was paid by the Metropolitian Museum of New York when they privately purchased a painted Greek urn of about 530 BC in August, 1972. By comparison, the highest price obtained at auction by a piece of English porcelain is £32,000, for a Chelsea tureen in the form of a boar's head, sold at Sotheby's in 1973. The auction record for a piece of English pottery is £15,015, for an eighteenth-century salt-glaze pew group, sold at Christie's in 1975.

Yet for all the beauty inherent in individual ceramic objects and for all the excitement of the auction, the study of pottery and porcelain must be kept in perspective. Let it be remembered that collecting is also a bug, albeit a delightful one, an acquisitive virus that once caught is unlikely to be cured. Collecting therefore requires the curb of your caution: above all, never let yourself be ruled by your possessions. Antiques have been collected for hundreds of years and many individuals have beggared themselves in the process, and it is for this reason, to prevent us from taking ourselves too seriously, that I recall a passage from Jerome K. Jerome's classic work of humour *Three Men in a Boat*, first published in 1889. 'I wonder if there is real intrinsic beauty in the old soup-plates, beer-mugs, and candle-snuffers that we prize so now, or if it is only the halo of age glowing around them that gives them their charms in our eyes. The "old blue" that we hang about our walls as ornaments were the common every-day household utensils of a few centuries ago; and the pink shepherds, and the yellow shepherdesses that we hand round now for all our friends to gush over, and pretend they understand, were the unvalued mantel-ornaments that the mother of the eighteenth century would have given the baby to suck when he cried.

'Will it be the same in the future? Will the prized treasures of today always be the cheap trifles of the day before? Will rows of our willow-pattern dinner-plates be ranged above the chimneypieces of the great in the year 2000 and odd? Will the white cups with the gold rim and the beautiful gold flower inside (species unknown), that our Sarah Janes now break in sheer light-heartedness of spirit, be carefully mended, and stood upon a bracket, and dusted only by the lady of the house? That china dog ornaments the bedroom of my furnished lodgings. It is a white dog. Its eyes are blue. Its nose is delicate red, with black spots. Its head is

17

painfully erect, and its expression is amiability carried to the verge of imbecility. I do not admire it myself. Considered as a work of art, I may say it irritates me. Thoughtless friends jeer at it, and even my landlady herself has no admiration for it, and excuses its presence by the circumstance that her aunt gave it to her.

'But in 200 years time it is more than probable that the dog will be dug up somewhere or other, minus its legs, and with its tail broken, and will be sold for old china, and put in a glass cabinet. And people will pass it round, and admire it. They will be struck by the wonderful depth of the colour on the nose, and speculate as to how beautiful the bit of the tail that is lost no doubt was.

9 White porcelain figure of a hound. Chelsea, *c.* 1749. Victoria and Albert Museum, London.

'We, in this age, do not see the beauty of that dog. We are too familiar with it. It is like the sunset and the stars: we are not awed by their loveliness because they are common to our eyes. So it is with that china dog. In 2288 people will gush over it. The making of such dogs will have become a lost art. Our descendants will wonder how we did it, and say how clever we were. We shall be referred to lovingly as those grand old artists that flourished in the nineteenth century, and produced those china dogs.

'The sampler that the eldest daughter did at school will be spoken of as tapestry of the Victorian era and be almost priceless. The blue-and-white mugs of the present-day roadside inn will be hunted up, all cracked and chipped, and sold for their weight in gold, and rich people will use them for claret cups; travellers from Japan will buy up all the Presents from Ramsgate and Souvenirs of Margate, that may of escaped destruction, and take them back to Jedo as ancient English curios . . .'

Many a true word is indeed uttered in jest, and I admire his observation that the eyes of his china dog are blue, for such apparently irrelevant detail can be of great help to the porcelain collector when dating objects. Very few English porcelain figure groups of the eighteenth century have so far been found with blue eyes; the majority are brown. Such information forms but a rule of thumb, but what an important one it is to have.

This observation brings us back to the other side of the coin in antique collecting: that it is a fascinating process, full of exciting discovery. It is the intention of this book to encourage you to look at pottery and porcelain with a fresh eye and to help you in the identification and basic understanding of the objects you will come to see and handle.

Chapter 2

Unravelling the mystique

No collector, or antique dealer for that matter, ever stops learning. The new collector in particular will be well advised to look at objects, examine them carefully, and try and absorb new facts all the time. The importance of actually handling pottery and porcelain cannot be over-emphasised. You may read all the relevant books, follow programmes on the radio and television, listen to lectures, but until you handle the pieces themselves none of the information you may have gained from these sources will ever fall properly into place. The following story will serve to illustrate how much can be gained by actually picking an object up and examining it carefully.

Many years ago, just before my sixteenth birthday, I attended an auction sale in a private house in Sussex. I knew nothing about ceramics beyond the fact that a plate was a plate, a vase was a vase, and if an object was called Ming it must therefore be old and valuable. The house had been the home of a porcelain collector, and during the course of that day my eyes were opened. I watched an elderly man lift a plate from a box of miscellaneous items and heard him mutter to a colleague 'Derby, about 1800'. When they had moved on I looked at the plate. It was painted with flowers but, apart from that, there was nothing to indicate who had made it, or where. I was puzzled and at the same time becoming quite desperate to know how anyone should be able to examine an object bearing no mark or label and yet apparently be quite certain of its origins. Later in the day when the sale was in progress I saw another plate, quite dull in appearance, white porcelain with a sketchy decoration in sepia and with slight touches of gold – to my utter astonishment that single plate fetched £30, which was more money than I had in the world. I looked at my catalogue and found the plate was described as 'eighteenth-century Chinese' with the word 'Jesuit' in inverted commas. The triumphant purchaser paid for the plate and carried it off immediately. I soon discovered exactly how this incident confirmed the importance of handling and understanding the porcelain itself: the majority of eighteenth-century pottery and porcelain is unmarked, and it was only during the nineteenth century that factories became more meticulous in marking products. This discovery disclosed to me a more than half hidden and entirely fascinating field of interest.

There are very many small points of observation that reveal so much of importance to the collector of ceramics, and it is difficult for the beginner to know what to look for. Pottery is generally easier than porcelain to understand, but varies in quality from simple earthenwares to formulae including clay, flint and other additives that produce sophisticated stonewares. Some stonewares, like Wedgwood's jasper ware, begin to approach porcelain in quality. However, most pottery is decidedly cheaper and far more simple to produce than porcelain. Early English porcelains, made at such places as Bow, Chelsea, Bristol, Plymouth and Worcester, were largely experimental. Each ceramic formula had methods of production creating various characteristics that are to be observed in shape, decoration, glaze and in the body of the porcelain itself. Coming to understand such characteristics is a long but compulsive process, making it eventually possible to examine an object, diagnose its distinguishing features, and so determine its place of manufacture, date and possibly even its modeller and decorator as well. A few remarks on Worcester porcelain will clarify this comment. It is for example a useful test to hold the object over a powerful electric light bulb—a table lamp without its shade is ideal—and observe the colouring that is transmitted through the porcelain by the light. You might expect the colour to be the whiteness of the porcelain reflected by the bulb, but instead you will find it to be a light green: a distinctive feature of much eighteenth-century Worcester.

Most porcelain items intended to be placed on tables have what is known as a foot-rim, the ridge on which the object stands, and it is this feature that will very often repay careful study. The foot-rim will often clearly indicate the nature of the porcelain used in the object's manufacture, and may also provide information concerning its glaze. Some factories also applied their marks to the inside of foot-rims, which is useful to know as these can sometimes be overlooked. A Worcester foot-rim will reveal, if looked at carefully, something of a 'cheesey' appearance, and the porcelain of which it is made is termed soft paste. This leads us to another interesting feature of Worcester. If you have ever read one of the many old books on

10 'Cistercian' ware vessel in the shape of a trumpet. This together with its glaze makes it typical of monastic wares made during the sixteenth century. Height 8¾ inches (222 mm). Museum of London.

11 Another typical medieval shape with a clear green glaze that was to remain popular throughout the Tudor period. Fifteenth century. Museum of London.

12 An imitation Wedgwood jasper ware teapot made by Neale & Co., 1780. British Museum, London.

13 The base of an eighteenth-century Worcester teapot, showing the irregular spread of the glaze and the narrow unglazed area just inside the foot-rim.

china collecting, you may well have found a statement to the effect that 'Worcester porcelain will usually show a dry edge on the inside of the foot-rim, caused by the retraction of the glaze'. While this dry edge as described is usually present, it is not caused by the reason stated. Glaze can only expand in the kiln, it does not shrink, retract or recoil. The Worcester dry edge was caused by the 'pegger' who, after the object had been dipped in glaze, used a small wooden peg to wipe away the excess within the foot-rim before the object was packed with its companions into saggers and loaded into the kiln for firing. This ensured that the minimum number of porcelain pieces adhered to each other, or to the sagger itself, so reducing the number of expensive breakages. When a Worcester piece is taken out of the kiln the dry edge is revealed as a result of the pegger's work, and the glaze left in the centre of the base will emerge with an irregular line and will in most cases fail to meet the edge of the foot-rim. This technique is an important one as the manufacture of porcelain is far more costly than that of pottery, particularly in the case of figure groups, where modelling, casting, assembling and decorating are all involved in the final result. The same characteristic also appears on objects from Caughley and on some of the Liverpool manufactories.

It is still not infrequent on view days in provincial sale rooms to notice a collector or dealer swiftly allowing the tip of his pencil to slide around the inside of the foot-rim of whatever he is looking at. If the pencil fails to draw a line then it is an immediate indication that the glaze is present across the entire base, whereas if a line is drawn it will show that the graphite in the pencil has crossed a surface of unglazed porcelain and could therefore well indicate an example of eighteenth-century Worcester. Such tests as these, however, valuable as they are, should never be accepted in isolation by the beginner, who should always check as many known characteristics as possible. It is particularly essential to follow this practice when you find objects bearing important eighteenth-century marks, for there are many fakes and copies in existence. Human nature being what it is, the sight of any mark will immediately blind many people to the fact that it might be something other than what it purports to be.

Broadly speaking there are two main categories of porcelain, referred to as hard paste and soft paste respectively. The essential distinction between them is, as their names would imply, one of hardness of substance. A different formula is used for hard paste, which is fired at a much higher temperature than soft paste porcelain. In the nineteenth century collectors carried with them as an aid to identification a file which would cut soft paste easily while making no impression on hard paste. Needless to say this is a practice that is severely frowned upon today, but if you want to see the differences for yourself try obtaining some damaged pieces of porcelain of both types. One thing that you will notice is that the chip in the soft paste has a granular texture not unlike that of a digestive biscuit, whereas hard paste presents a surface that is flint- or glass-like in appearance. Lead glaze is used on most soft paste porcelains, whereas the glaze on hard paste items is sometimes of stone. Lead glaze also tends to gather and pool on a figure, for example, where the bend of an arm or the fold of clothes permits it. This does not occur with glazes made from china stone.

The Chinese, who made the world's first porcelain, did so according to a hard paste formula consisting of china stone (known as petuntse) and china clay (known as kaolin), and produced pieces of outstanding quality. The same formula was discovered in Germany at the beginning of the eighteenth

14 Liverpool transfer printed coffee pot. The shape is typical.

century: the commercial success of the Meissen factory, the popularity of Oriental porcelain imports and consequent decline of interest in earthenware led to intensive experiments into porcelain manufacture. Because of the failure of experimenters to find a harder paste, a number of soft paste porcelains were evolved around this time; English factories in particular, with a few exceptions, used soft paste.

Soft paste has the same attribute of translucency as hard paste but is technically inferior as it is less stable in the kiln. This meant that soft paste figures were difficult to fire; they needed to be propped while in the kiln and lacked the vitality and freedom of the hard paste figures of Meissen. Modelling was therefore restricted. Thus manufacturers were always attempting to produce a harder paste in the knowledge that soft paste was second best. However, generations of collectors will testify that soft paste porcelains have a unique and distinctive charm that will become apparent if the reader perseveres in studying and handling them.

Once the substance of porcelain had been manufactured, it then needed to be shaped into objects of everyday use such as bowls, cups and plates, or into decorative figure models. The next stage was decoration. At first, many pieces of European porcelain were left entirely white, mainly because a tradition of porcelain decoration did not exist in Europe. As we have already noted, Chinese porcelains were well known in Europe long before the method of porcelain manufacture was discovered in the Western world, and it is therefore not surprising that early European porcelains should derive their style of decoration from Oriental sources. In particular, the direct copying or the basing of designs upon known Chinese originals was an obvious step. Most of the English manufacturers of porcelain favoured, particularly in the early stages of their development, the use of blue-and-white decoration. The study and collection of English blue-and-white porcelain of the eighteenth century is a most attractive and stimulating pursuit although, sadly, becoming more costly as each year goes by.

Porcelain decorations in enamel colours (that is, colours which are applied over the glaze) are naturally more striking and have a lustrous appearance. This is particularly so with specimens painted with Oriental figures. In years past many an uninformed country auctioneer sold English porcelain so decorated as Oriental examples, which gives strength to my previous comment that a firm knowledge of the type of porcelain of which the object is made is vital if proper identification is to be achieved. The Oriental style of enamel figure painting, whether carried out at Worcester, Liverpool or New Hall, has a unique quality that is frequently missed by the beginner. Look at, say, a Chinese cup of the late eighteenth century and compare it carefully with its English counterpart. At first glance they both appear to be entirely Oriental, but ignore for a moment the clothing and the background which help to produce the overall effect, and concentrate instead upon the faces. With most of the examples that are examined in this way you will find a subtle difference. The English specimen, while capturing the spirit of the original, usually fails to reflect accurately the Oriental features and the result is more often a face of somewhat Eurasian appearance.

So far in this chapter, we have described the basic materials from which porcelain is made, and the stages it goes through, such as the decoration, before the finished product is achieved, and it is hoped that this will be useful information for the reader to keep in the back of his mind as specific objects and their manufacture are described. It will also be useful to clarify at this point certain confusions arising from the profusion of names used in the study of pottery and porcelain. For a start, the same name can be applied to both the fabric that is used for making an object and the object itself: thus 'porcelain' can mean both the material and the thing or things made out of it. Another difficulty is that during the course of the importation of ceramic objects into this country, many generic terms came to be applied which are inexact and confusing. China, for example, is a word in daily use, but what exactly does it mean? In the next few pages I shall give a brief sketch of the history of the importation of the porcelain objects into this country, in the course of which the different names used will, it is hoped, become clearer.

The main passion for collecting in Britain developed during the reign of William III, and a large collection of Oriental wares and Dutch Delft decorated in the Oriental manner was established by Queen Mary at Kensington Palace; an inventory of this collection was drawn up in 1696. For many people this ceramic enthusiasm became an obsession, and Daniel Defoe writes of finding china '. . . upon the tops of cabinets, scrutores and every chimney piece to the tops of the ceilings . . . till it became a grievance in the expense of it and was injurious to their families and Estates.'

Among the larger decorative porcelains to be imported from the Orient were groups of vases known as *garniture de cheminée*, usually consisting of three covered vases and two beakers. Other imports consisted of items of European design

15 Staffordshire slipware portrait dish depicting William III (1689-1702). The dish is large having a diameter of 16¾ inches (420 mm). Victoria and Albert Museum, London.

16 Delftware plate painted in blue and yellow also depicting William III and Mary II. Probably Lambeth, 1691. Ashmolean Museum, Oxford, Warren Collection.

17 Delftware portrait dish depicting Charles II. Painted mainly in blue with some yellow, brown, orange and purple. Note the blue-dash border, a typical feature of such pieces. Probably Lambeth, 1661. Birmingham Museums and Art Gallery, A. C. J. Wall loan.

24

manufactured in China, blue-and-white porcelain entirely Oriental in decoration and design, and blue-and-white porcelain brought to Europe for additional decoration. These latter pieces are now referred to as 'clobbered' wares, and although interesting they are usually highly unsatisfactory in appearance. Some examples of Oriental porcelain were brought to Europe 'in the white' for decoration here, but these are not common. Most of the later Chinese porcelains decorated in polychrome (many colour) enamels are described as Canton, for it was in that city on the Pearl River that most of the enamelling was done. Similarly the later blue-and-white Chinese export pieces are termed Nankin, for this was the port from which most were exported. These names, together with the fact that most wares were brought to Europe in the ships of the various nations' East India companies, resulted in India and China being used as generic terms for Far Eastern wares. In due course the word 'china' in England came to describe virtually anything of a ceramic nature, just as the term 'japanned' and 'Indian' were applied to furniture lacquered anywhere in the Far East during the seventeenth and eighteenth centuries.

In the nineteenth century it was firmly believed that large imports of Chinese porcelain in the white had been delivered in the eighteenth century to the Lowestoft porcelain works and decorated there. Hence yet another confusing term: 'Chinese Lowestoft'. In fact products given this name were both made and decorated in China and are true export wares, and yet in many circles, particularly in America, this misnomer still flourishes.

Individuals who imported or sold china were described as chinamen. One such man was Miles Mason, who also established a family manufacturing business renowned for its highly popular Mason's ironstone. His business as a wholesale and retail dealer in Oriental porcelain became impossible to carry on due to the Napoleonic wars, but the following advertisement which he placed in the *London Morning Herald* of 15 October 1804 not only illuminates some of the comments already made in this chapter, but also demonstrates the character and initiative of the man:

'It has hitherto been the opinion, not only of the Public, but also of the Manufacturers of this Country that the Earths of these Kingdoms are unequal to those of Foreign Nations for the fabrication of China. Miles Mason, late of Fenchurch Street, London, having been a principal purchaser of Indian Porcelain, till the prohibition of that article by heavy duties, has established a Manufactory at Lane Delph, near

Newcastle-under-Line [sic], upon the principle of the Indian and Sève [sic] China. The former is now sold at the principal Shops only in the City of London and the Country as British Nankin. His article is warranted from the Manufactory to possess superior qualities to Indian Nankin China, being more beautiful as well as more durable, and not so liable to snip at the edges, more difficult to break, and refusable or unitable by heat, if broken. Being aware that to combat strong prejudices with success, something superior must be produced: he, therefore, through the medium of his Wholesale Friends, proposes to renew or match the impaired or broken services of the Nobility and Gentry, when by fair trial or conjunction with foreign china, he doubts not that these fears will be removed, and, in a short period, the Manufactories of Porcelain, by the patronage of the Nobility of this country, will rival, if not excel, those of foreign Nations.

N.B. The articles are stamped on the bottom of the large pieces to prevent imposition.'

In 1736 a treatise published in France gave enormous encouragement to the endeavours of the European porcelain pioneers. The paper, *A Description of the Empire of China and of*

18 A fine Miles Mason porcelain teapot. The small impressed name mark, 'M. Mason', is just visible on the rim of the base.

Chinese Tartary, included considerable detail of the manufacturing methods and materials used by the Chinese in their production of hard paste porcelain. The information had mainly come from some long, detailed and very charming letters written in 1712 by a Jesuit missionary known as Père d'Entrecolles. The following extracts from these letters are not only interesting for their historic worth, but also help the beginner to understand the nature of porcelain and the various processes which it undergoes during manufacture:

'From time to time I have stayed in Ching-tê-chên to administer to the spiritual necessities of my converts, and so I have interested myself in the manufacture of this beautiful porcelain, which is so highly prized, and is sent to all parts of the world. Nothing but my curiosity could ever have prompted me to such researches, but it appears to me that a minute description of all that concerns this kind of work might, somehow, be useful in Europe.

'Besides what I myself have seen, I have learnt a great many particulars from my neophytes, several of whom work in porcelain, while others do a great trade in it. I also confirmed the truth of the information they had given me by a study of the Chinese books on the subject, so that I believe I have obtained a pretty exact knowledge of all that concerns this beautiful art, so that I can talk about it with some confidence.'

'The material of porcelain is composed of two kinds of clay, one called Pe-tun-tse and the other Kao-lin. The latter is disseminated with corpuscles which have some shimmer, the former is simply white and very fine to the touch. While a large number of big boats come up the river from Jao-chou to Ching-tê-chên to be loaded with porcelain, nearly as many small ones come down from Ki-mên laden with Pe-tun-tse and Kao-lin made up into bricks, for Ching-tê-chên does not produce any of the materials suitable for porcelain. Pe-tun-tse, which is so fine in grain, is simply pulverized rock taken from quarries, and then shaped into bricks. Every kind of stone is not suitable, or it would not be necessary to go for it, twenty or thirty miles away, into the next province. The good stone, the Chinese say, must have a slight tinge of green. The pieces of stone are first broken with iron hammers, and the fragments are reduced to a very fine powder in mortars by means of certain levers which have a stone head shod with iron. These levers are worked incessantly, either by men or by water-power, in the same way as the tilt-hammers in paper-mills. The powder is then put into a great vessel filled with water, and stirred vigorously with an iron shovel. When it has been allowed to stand several minutes, a kind of cream forms at the top four or five fingers thick; this they take off and put into another vessel full of water. The mixture in the first vessel is stirred up several times, and each time they remove the scum that gathers on the top, until nothing is left but the larger particles, the weight of which makes them sink to the bottom; these are finally taken out and again pounded. With regard to the second vessel into which they put all that has been skimmed out of the first, they wait until a kind of paste has formed at the bottom, and when the water above it seems very clear it is poured off so as not to disturb the sediment. This paste is then thrown into moulds which are a kind of large and wide wooden box, the bottom of which is a bed of bricks with an even surface. Over this brick bed a coarse cloth is stretched, up to the sides of the case; this cloth is filled with the paste, and soon afterwards they cover it with another cloth on the top of which they put a layer of bricks laid evenly, one by the side of the other. This helps to squeeze out the water more quickly without losing any of the porcelain material which, as it hardens readily, takes the shape of the bricks. Before it has become quite hard the paste is divided into little bricks, which are sold by the hundred; this colour and the shape have given it the name Pe-tun-tse. There would be nothing to add to this preparation if the Chinese were not in the habit of adulterating their merchandise; but people who roll little grains of paste in pepper dust, and mix them with real peppercorns, are not likely to sell Pe-tun-tse without mixing it with coarser materials, so that it has to be purified afresh before it is used.

'Kao-lin requires a little less labour than Pe-tun-tse; nature has done the greater part. Mines of it are found in the heart of certain mountains, which on the outside are covered with reddish earth. These mines are fairly deep; it is found there in masses, and it is also made up into little squares in the same method as described above for the Pe-tun-tse. I should be inclined to think that the white clay of Malta, known as the clay of St Paul, approaches in its nature to the Kao-lin I am speaking of, although one cannot perceive in it the small silvery particles with which the Kao-lin is sown. Fine porcelain owes its strength to the Kao-lin; it is only the mixture of a soft earth or a soft clay which gives strength to the Pe-tun-tse obtained from the hardest rocks.

'A rich merchant told me that the English or Dutch (the Chinese use the same name for both nations) bought, several years ago, some Pe-tun-tse, which they took to their own country to make porcelain with, but, having taken no Kao-lin, their undertaking failed, as they afterwards owned. The Chinese merchant said to me, laughing, "They wanted to have a body without bones to support its flesh".'

'For the fine porcelains they put as much Kao-lin as Pe-tun-tse; for the inferior ones they use four parts of Kao-lin and six parts of Pe-tun-tse; while the least that they use is one part of Kao-lin and three of Pe-tun-tse.

'The mixture is thrown into a big pit well paved and cemented, where it is trodden and kneaded until it becomes stiff; this is very laborious work; those Christians who are employed at it find it difficult to attend church; they are only allowed to go if they can find substitutes, because as soon as this work is interrupted all other workmen are stopped.

'From the mass thus prepared, lumps are taken and spread on large slates. The workmen knead, beat, and roll them thoroughly, taking care that no hollows are left inside the mass and that no foreign bodies get into it A hair, a grain of sand would spoil the whole work. If this mass is badly worked the porcelain cracks, splits, drops or bends. From these prime materials such beautiful works of porcelain are produced, some by shaping on the wheel, others only in moulds; and they are afterwards finished with a knife. All the plain pieces are made in the first way. A cup, for example, when it leaves the wheel, is very roughly shaped, almost like the top of a hat before it has been blocked. The first workman only gives it the required diameter and height, and it leaves his hands almost as soon as it is commenced, for he receives only three 'deniers' per board, and on each board are twenty-six pieces. The foot of the cup is then nothing but a piece of clay of the necessary width, and it is only hollowed out with a knife when the other operations are finished, and when the cup is dry and firm enough. When the cup leaves the wheel it is taken by a second workman, who puts it straight upon its base. Shortly afterwards it is handed over to a third man, who puts it on its mould and gives it its shape; this mould is mounted on a kind of wheel. A fourth workman trims and polishes the cup, especially the rims, with a knife, and pares it down as much as necessary for its transparency; he scrapes it several times and moistens each time, however little he may have pared it, if it is too dry, for fear he should break it. In taking the cup from the mould they turn it softly on the same mould without pressing it more on one side than the other, otherwise it would only pass for apprentices of a few months' standing. All the science of these painters, and of Chinese painters in general, is based on no principles, and only consists in a certain routine helped by a limited turn of imagination. They of seventy workmen. I can easily believe this by what I have myself seen, for these great workshops have been for me a kind of Areopagus, where I have preached Him who fashioned the first men out of clay, and from whose hands we depart to become vessels of honour or of shame.'

'It is time to ennoble the porcelain by passing it over into the hands of the painters. These porcelain painters are not less poor and wretched than the other workmen, which is not very surprising when we remember that in Europe they would only pass for apprentices of a few months' standing. All the science of these painters, and of Chinese painters in general, is based on no principles, and only consists in a certain routine helped by a limited turn of imagination. They know nothing of the beautiful rules of this art; though it must be acknowledged that they paint flowers, animals, and landscapes which are much admired, on porcelain as well as on fans and lanterns of the finest gauze. The painting is distributed in the same workshop among a great number of workmen. One workman does nothing but draw the first colour line beneath the rims of the pieces; another traces flowers, which a third one paints; this man is painting water and mountains, and that one either birds or other animals. Human figures are generally treated the worst. Certain landscapes and plans of towns that are brought over from Europe to China will hardly allow us, however, to mock at the Chinese for the manner in which they represent themselves in their paintings.'

'When they wish to apply gold they beat it and grind it in water in a porcelain dish until they see underneath the water a little golden cloud. This they leave to dry, and in use they mix it with a sufficiency of gum-water, and with thirty parts of gold they incorporate three parts of white lead, and put it on the porcelain in the same way as the colours.'

'Great skill is required in putting the glaze on to the

porcelain so that it is not too thick, and that it is evenly spread over the piece. For porcelain pieces that are very thin and light, they apply two slight coats of glaze. If the coats of glaze are too thick the thin sides of the vessel cannot support them, and will instantly sink out of shape. These two layers are equal to one ordinary layer of glaze such as is put on the thicker pieces. The first coating is put on by sprinkling, the other by immersion. The cup is held in the hand from outside, sloping over the vessel that contains the glaze, and with the other hand they pour inside as much glaze as is needed to wet it everywhere. This is done to a great many cups, and when the first ones are dry inside, the glaze is put on the outside as follows: The workman puts one hand into the cup, and, supporting it with a little stick under the middle of its foot, he dips it into the vessel filled with glaze, and quickly draws it out again.'

'I have been surprised to see how a man can balance on his shoulders two long and narrow planks on which the porcelain pieces are carried, and that he goes like that through several well-populated streets without breaking his ware. It is true that the people carefully avoid knocking against him, however slightly, because they would be obliged to pay for the damage they had caused, but it is astonishing that the carrier himself controls his steps and all the movements of his body so well that he does not lose his balance.

'Where the furnaces are we find another scene. In a kind of vestibule before the furnace one sees piles of boxes and cases made of clay prepared for holding the porcelain. Each vase of porcelain, however small it may be, has its case; the pieces that have covers as well as those that have none–these covers are only slightly attached to the bottom part during the firing, so that they easily come apart by a little blow. The small porcelain pieces, like tea- and chocolate-cups, are placed a good many in one case. In this operation the workman imitates Nature, who to ripen the fruit and bring it to perfection, puts it into a case so that the heat of the sun gets at it little by little, and its action inside is not too much interfered with by the air that comes from outside during the fresh nights.

'These cases [saggers] are lined with a kind of sand-down, for they are covered with "kao-lin" dust as this sand does not stick too much to the foot of the piece that is put on it. The bed of sand is first pressed and given the shape of the bottom of the porcelain piece, which does not itself touch the sides of its case. The top of the case has no lid; a second case, after the shape of the first and similarly filled with porcelain, comes on it, so that it covers it completely without touching the porcelain underneath. In this way they fill the kiln with big cases all containing porcelain. Thanks to these thick veils the beauty, and, if I may say so, the complexion of the porcelain piece is not sunburnt by the heat of the fire.'

After reading these descriptions it would be helpful to visit the English potteries and tour some of the modern factories, for it is interesting that the basic philosophy and skills have remained remarkably similar.

In England the man upon whom the letters of Père d'Entre-colles were to have most impact was William Cookworthy (1705-1780), a young Quaker apothecary living in Plymouth. Having read the letters, he spent many years searching the West Country for the materials he saw described as kaolin and petuntse; in fact he had already seen the materials earlier in his life but had been unable then to appreciate their significance. Light finally dawned upon him when he was visited by a man named André Duché. Duché had arrived from North America where his Huguenot parents had settled following the Revoca-tion of the Edict of Nantes in 1685. His experiments with china clay and china stone enabled Cookworthy to see what was required and a letter to his friend Dr Richard Hingstone, a fellow Quaker living at Penryn, demonstrates his enthusiasm. 'I had lately with me (1744) the person who has discovered the China Earth. He had with him several samples of the china ware, which, I think, were equal to the Asiatic. It was found on the back of Virginia, where he was in quest of mines, and having read Du Halde, he discovered both the Petunse and the Caulin [sic]. He is gone for a cargo of it, having bought from the Indians the whole country where it rises. They can import it for £13 per ton, and by that means afford their China as cheap as common stoneware; but they intend only to go about 30% under the Company.'
Cookworthy then launched into an enterprise to set up a porcelain works in Bristol, but it appears to have failed because Duché was unable to guarantee the regular supply of clay from Virginia, probably due to the flimsy nature of his agreements with the Indians on whose lands he mined.

Cookworthy's efforts successfully to identify and obtain the essential ingredients of porcelain in Cornwall bore rich fruit, but his attempts to manufacture porcelain were beset with difficulties. In a letter to Dr Hingstone he writes:

'I am at a loss to know best how to set about the work of producing porcelain of a fit and proper nature. I have the caulin [sic], which is the best that can be had, and I have the petunse [sic], which I think is equal to the Chinese, and with these two I have both the flesh, the bones and the sinews, but to put flesh on bone to make a whole body, that is what perplexes me. There are times when I think that I shall, God willing, succeed in this enterprise, and other times when I wonder if 'tis destined for me to succeed.'

However, on 17 March 1768 William Cookworthy's Patent for the manufacture of porcelain was issued, part of which reads:

'Now know ye that I, the said William Cookworthy, do by this my deed in writing, declare the nature of my said invention and the quality of the materials and the manner in which the same is performed, which is as followeth:—

''The materials of which the body of the said porcelain is composed are a stone and earth or clay. The stone is known in the counties of Devon & Cornwall by the names of moorstone and growan, which stones are generally composed of grains of stone or gravel of a white or whitish colour, with a mixture of talcy shining particles. This gravel and these particles are cemented together by a petrified clay into very solid rocks, and immense quantities of them are found in both the above mentioned counties. All these stones, exposed to a violent fire, melt without the addition of fluxes into a semi-transparent glass, differing in clearness and beauty according to the purity of the stone. The earth or clay, for the most part, lies in the valleys where the stone forms the hills. This earth is frequently very white, though sometimes of a yellowish or cream colour. It generally arises with a large mixture of talcy mica or spangles and a semi-transparent whitish gravel. Some sorts have little or none of the mica or spangles, but the best clay for making porcelain always abounds in mica or spangles. The stone is prepared by levigation, in a potter's mill in water, in the usual way, to a very fine powder. The clay is prepared by diluting it with water until the mixture is rendered sufficiently thin for the gravel and mica to subside, the white water containing the clay is then poured or left to run off from the subsided mica and gravel into proper vessels or reservoirs, and after it has settled for a day or two, the clear water above it is to be then poured or drawn off, and the clay or earth reduced to a proper consistence by the common methods of exposing it to the sun and air, or laying it on chalk. This earth or clay gives the ware its whiteness and infusibility as the stone doth its transparence and mellowness; they are therefore to be mixed in different proportions as the ware is intended to be more or less transparent, and the mixture is to be performed in the method used by potters and well known (viz. by diluting the materials in water, passing the mixture through a fine sieve and reducing it to a paste of a proper consistence for working, in the way directed for the preparation of the clay). This paste is to be formed into vessels, and these vessels when biscuited are to be dipped in the glaze, which is prepared of the levigated stone with the addition of lime and fern ashes, or an earth called magnesia alba, in such quantities as may make it properly fusible and transparent when it has received a due degree of fire in the second baking.''   WILLIAM L. S. COOKWORTHY'

Cookworthy later transferred his manufactory from Plymouth to Bristol, and in 1774 he assigned his patent to Richard Champion. When Champion lodged his application for an extension to the original patent in 1775 it was bitterly opposed by Josiah Wedgwood who himself needed to obtain supplies of china clay. After prolonged legal negotiations Champion's patent was severely pruned and this, together with his legal costs, made it almost impossible for him to continue in business. Later, in December 1780, he formed another small company which bought the patent from him and carried on the production of hard paste porcelain similar to the original Cookworthy formula. This company came to be known as the New Hall Co. of Shelton. Further mention of Plymouth, Bristol and New Hall will be found in Chapter 6.

Many variations of formula were used in the production of soft paste. Often it consisted of calcined flint with sand and potash or lead mixed with china clay, which therefore replaced china stone. This type of body, something of a glassy mixture, is termed frit. Other factories substituted soapstone from Cornwall which produced a far more satisfactory soft paste body, enabling very fine potting to be carried out. The soapstone, or steatite body as it is called, was fired in the kiln at a lower temperature than either the hard paste or the frit bodies, and was also commercially attractive in that the products were less subject to cracking or warping.

Even more successful was the bone ash body developed by the addition of calcined ox-bones to soft paste materials. The Bow factory was the first to experiment successfully with calcined bone. When calcined ox-bones were added to the hard paste formula at the end of the eighteenth century, thus creating the now familiar bone china, it was a major break-through in commercial production. Josiah Spode was a pioneer in this respect, and in the early nineteenth century many other factories, including Worcester, Derby, Coalport and Minton, were quick to adopt it. Bone china produced a body of very high translucency that continues to be greatly admired today and is the basic formula for modern porcelain production in England. Felspar china takes its name from the addition of felspar to the bone china formula, at the same time using less china stone. This again resulted in a body that behaved well in the kiln, together with the commercial attributes of trans-lucency and the ability to withstand hard use.

Many confusing names are to be found in the marks of nineteenth-century earthenware, and such terms as semi-porcelain, opaque porcelain, ironstone and stone china are all improved earthenwares and should not be mistaken for porcelain. The majority of porcelain tablewares are easily shown to be translucent and this is, of course, one of the essential qualities of porcelain; the earthenwares always being opaque and usually requiring a glaze to make them impermeable by water.

Once more it is necessary to stress the necessity of handling the products of as many factories as possible in order to be able to recognise the characteristics of the ceramic bodies used. An old friend, a medical practitioner in Wales, once told me how, when caring for an elderly member of a family he had attended for many years, he was surprised to find the family gathered in the hallway one day in order to make a presentation to him before he left. The doctor, having collected porcelain for most of his life, had always noted the cabinets of fine china in this particular house and the family had told him that their greatest treasure was a Chelsea mug on a very high shelf. He had admired the mug frequently, but it was never lifted down for handling. However, the gift they now handed him was nothing less than their treasured Chelsea mug. The doctor described the sense of pleasure and excitement as he reached out to accept it, 'but' he said 'I hope my face did not betray my change of feelings, or my voice my sense of gratitude. As it came into my hands I realised that what I was holding was a French hard paste copy of a Chelsea mug made by Samson of Paris in the nineteenth century.' It is rather a sad story but it does emphas-ise the value of understanding the porcelain itself through a careful handling rather than being merely beguiled by attrac-tive decoration and a false mark, in this case a spurious gold anchor.

Chapter 3

The influences from abroad

English pottery and porcelain in the initial stages of its development was particularly influenced by Oriental shapes and patterns and also to some extent by products from the Continent. The most influential country, so far as the ceramic arts are concerned, is, as will have been apparent from the outset, China.

The Chinese revered porcelain second only to jade. It bore many of the attributes inherent in this hard stone: for example it was hard, pure and translucent and had a musical note when struck. This delight in the material for its own sake has resulted in the finest objects ever made in porcelain coming from China. Nor should our appreciation of this fact be obscured by European misuse of their decorative patterns. It was only in the nineteenth century that the Chinese became increasingly guilty of over-decoration, and much of that was due to the demands of the European market. Traditionally Chinese

19 Delftware dish painted in blue, red, green and yellow. Note the rather elongated female figures, which are known in Dutch as 'Lange Lijzen' and in English as 'Long Elizas'. Bristol, 1733. City Art Gallery, Bristol.

ceramics reflected Chinese religious beliefs and culture, and a whole panorama of their gods and immortals was paraded on their porcelain, which was also decorated with emblems reflecting other aspects of life. To understand the meaning of Chinese decoration it is therefore necessary to have some knowledge of Taoism and Buddhism. The early potters and decorators in England lacked this knowledge and the result is that Oriental emblems are frequently mixed in a most extraordinary manner, attention being paid only to their decorative effect and their cultural implications being ignored.

Thus while some of the Oriental designs were closely followed, the majority suffered badly at the hands of the potters, who seemed to have been most anxious to anglicise them. For example, the Chinese differentiated between ordinary dragons, which were painted with only three claws on each foot, and imperial dragons, which had five: such niceties as these were totally ignored by English painters. Pagodas begin to look more like European follies or outbuildings, seated Chinamen in their broad brimmed hats develop into giant toadstools, and trees and birds become stylised formalities.

One Oriental pattern to become very popular in Britain was the Imari. These porcelains, largely decorated with floral motifs, were made in the Hizen province of Japan, at the Arita kilns celebrated as the home of the Kakiemon family, of whom more later. The Arita kilns had begun production in the early seventeenth century and part of their output was termed Imari simply because it was shipped from the port of that name. They are recognised by the distinctive Imari palette with its dark underglaze blue, its strong red, and its gilding, which is sometimes overdone.

The Dutch were the principal traders with Japan and it was they who encouraged the Japanese decorators to copy designs from brocades and other textiles. Similar brocaded patterns were used by the English factories of Chelsea, Derby, Davenport, Worcester and many others; in fact various Japan patterns after the Imari style remained popular throughout the nineteenth century until the present day, the Derby Japan patterns being an excellent example of this.

The Chinese also manufactured the Imari patterns and technically their porcelain surpasses that of the Japanese. The glaze of the former is thinner and clearer while that of the Japanese often has a pitted muslin-like appearance.

The Kakiemon family worked at Arita. The patterns ascribed to them are highly sophisticated, using a palette that included only a slight gilding, as well as red, light blue, yellow and a distinctive bluish green. Figures, whether human or insect, were executed with a precise charm, as was the floral decoration, and all designs were carefully related to the shape of the vessel being decorated. The use of pattern is restrained and the overall shape and colour of the porcelain speaks for itself.

The Bow factory made great use of the well-known Kakiemon quail pattern around 1750, as did the Worcester factory later in the century. Worcester also used other patterns in the Kakiemon style, such as the Bengal tiger, and Chelsea used the beautiful narrative decoration that we call 'Hob in the Well'. These pieces are rare, and those marked with the Chelsea raised or red anchor dating from around 1752 are most highly prized. The 'Hob in the Well' pattern tells the story of a young boy who saves his even smaller friend from drowning by hurling a stone and smashing the massive fish bowl into which his friend had fallen.

20 Leaf-moulded porcelain dish, with a quail pattern after the Japanese Kakiemon style. Bow, 1755.

A distinguished ceramicist friend of mine noticed recently, in the window of a Surrey antique shop, a plate that appeared to be in the Kakiemon style. On entering the shop and expressing his interest in the plate he was quickly told by the dealer that while he too thought it was most attractive he only regretted that it was Japanese and not Chelsea. The plate was promptly purchased for just over three pounds, the jubilant purchaser leaving the antique shop with a superb specimen of seventeenth-century Japanese ceramic art.

Trade with the Far East had enabled English potters to become well acquainted with the various techniques of decoration available. The colour most widely used among the early English factories was underglaze blue. Derived from cobalt oxide, cobalt blue, the finest underglaze blue, is a colouring agent varying in range of tone from a greyish blue through blackish blue to its ultimate, sapphire. The variation in colour largely depended upon the quality of the cobalt ore used.

21 The underside of a Chelsea dish with a shaped edge, showing the 'stilt marks' where it was separated from its neighbours in the kiln, and, towards the edge, the raised anchor mark.

Cobalt blue was first developed in Persia from where it was rapidly introduced into China some time between the mid-thirteenth and mid-fourteenth centuries. The colour was therefore well established by the Ming dynasty (1368–1644 AD), and full use of it was made by the brilliant potters of that time. Further exports between China and the Middle East later led to several hundred Chinese potters settling in Persia with their families, thus enhancing Middle Eastern pottery.

Cobalt blue was well-suited as a colour for use under the glaze on English soft paste porcelain. The term 'underglaze' simply means that the colour used as decoration develops at the same time as the firing of the glaze. Any colour that is underglazed cannot be touched with the fingers, which means that any underglaze mark immediately indicates that it cannot have been applied to an object later than its manufacture. All overglaze marks should be examined with more care than usual as these will possibly have been added later. Caution should also be exercised whenever an unglazed area is found on the base of any porcelain object where a mark could reasonably be expected. It is not unknown for marks to be removed with acid or an abrasive wheel. This usually indicates that the mark had denoted a lesser manufactory than a previous owner had wished to admit to.

Various marks described as 'pseudo-Oriental' have been used from time to time on English porcelain and due attention has been given to these in the many excellent hand-books and encyclopaedias of marks now available.

Overglaze or 'on-glaze' decoration again means exactly what the name would imply—a decoration painted or printed on to the glazed surface of the object. The colours used in such decoration are enamel and are fixed in an enamelling kiln; and the decoration so formed can usually be felt with the fingers.

Beautifully coloured birds were made in China throughout the seventeenth and eighteenth centuries and there was a very ready market for these in Europe. Some copies of these exotic birds were made in porcelain, but other excellent models were made by Thomas Whieldon and other early eighteenth-century English potters. Later designs of birds painted on porcelain tend to depict either exotic birds copied from the Chinese, or to follow the European tradition of accurate bird and botanical painting.

Many Oriental shapes were taken up in England, most of which were the octagonal, hexagonal and straight-sided vessels introduced by the Far Eastern potters to provide added strength to the objects, usually vases or small bowls. Oriental bottle shapes with their bulbous bodies and tall narrow necks also found favour in England although the delightful double gourd shapes much used by the Japanese were copied far more frequently on the Continent than in England.

Much armorial porcelain, table services decorated with family monograms or coats of arms, was manufactured in China for English customers, and today such pieces are avidly collected, a fact clearly reflected in their value. Although excellent armorial ware was manufactured in England by most of the leading factories from 1750, the bulk of the orders for services and individual pieces went to China. Sketches, paintings, even bookplates, were forwarded to the Far East in order that the

arms might be accurately represented. So meticulous were the Chinese in their ability to copy such things that the waiting list was formidable. An outstanding example of this ware was shown to me some time ago: a Chinese tea service with each piece bearing the arms of the family, although only the outline of the arms and their supporters were visible. A sketch had been despatched to China showing the arms with the words blue, red, and so on, added where appropriate to show the colouring required. Unfortunately for the family concerned, the service arrived in England with no heraldic colours whatever – only the outlines as sketched with the words for the colours written in as on the original sketch. Today, of course, such a service is a great rarity!

The Chinese loved to keep fish in porcelain tanks superbly decorated on the inside. The most colourful of these date from the eighteenth century. The enamel decoration depicts weeds and water insects of all kinds, usually with carp and other fish painted in iron red. When seen through the rippled water in a full tank the fish appear almost alive. Many of these fish bowls and tanks are to be found in England and they clearly became popular from the 1750s. Smaller versions were also produced, sometimes in the form of punch-bowls, and the best of these are to be found in Liverpool Delft, where the fish are painted in blue on a manganese ground.

Delft takes its name from the Dutch town that became such a major centre for these well-known and now highly collectable tin-glazed wares, although it is to the Arab world, which provided another major influence on English and Continental

22 *Far left:* Delftware bottle-shape vase or water bottle, painted in enamel colours. Liverpool, 1750-60. Fitzwilliam Museum, Cambridge.

23 *Above:* Delftware wall pocket in the shape of a cornucopia and decorated in polychrome. Liverpool, *c.* 1760. Merseyside County Museum, Liverpool.

24 *Opposite:* 'The Goatherd'. A fine English hard paste porcelain figure. Bristol, *c.* 1775. Fenton House, Hampstead.

25 *Below:* The tiger and bamboo pattern, one of many Oriental patterns popular in England. On the left is the Japanese original and on the right the Chelsea version.

26 *Bottom:* Interesting examples of English hard paste porcelain.

The cream jug and teapot on the left are Bristol, the beaker vase and sauceboat on the right are Plymouth.

27 *Opposite, top:* A two-handled covered pot (right), and a heart-shaped toilet box (left). Chelsea, 1760-65. British Museum, London.

28 *Opposite, bottom:* A very fine early Worcester teapot decorated in the Oriental manner (left), and a Worcester chocolate cup and saucer (right) with paintings of fruit and apple-green borders.

ceramics, that we are indebted for the introduction of Delft into Europe. English Delft is discussed in the next chapter, but the background and development of the glaze belongs here.

Oxide of tin (stannic oxide to give it its real name) produces a glaze of opaque white enamel and, as far as is known, it was first used as a coating for building bricks in ancient Babylon and Nineveh. When the Moors conquered much of Spain in the late eleventh century they also introduced tin glazing into Europe. Many of their tiles glazed in this manner are still to be seen *in situ* in the Alhambra in Granada. Tin glazed objects in Spain are termed Hispano-Moresque wares, and their design has been much influenced by Islamic art.

Italian tin glazing is known as Maiolica and was already known in Italy by the fourteenth century. Luca della Robia, the Florentine sculptor who was born in 1400, used tin glaze many times during his career and it was in his lifetime that enthusiasm for the glaze really developed in Italy. The principal Italian towns producing Maiolica were Urbino, Gubbio, Castel Durante and Faenza, and the products of these towns are now much collected.

The success of the glaze largely stemmed from the fact that it was exceedingly dense and hard, and therefore comparatively poor clays could be used with it. This also provided an ideal background for decoration. As with most materials, however, there were also drawbacks. The soft clay provides little support for its hard tin glazed shell, and for this reason some degree of chipping is inevitable with this type of ware.

Holland undoubtedly became the leading centre in Northern Europe for tin glazed pottery, which reached the peak of its popularity in the late seventeenth century. The commercial success of Delftware led to an increasing demand for it in Britain. This stimulated the establishment of potteries for Delft production in several parts of England, Scotland and Ireland.

In Italy large dishes and wet and dry drug jars comprised much of the Maiolica output. In England the apothecaries were quick to realise the importance of tin glaze, its fine surface being ideal for their purposes. As well as small and humble ointment pots, truly noble drug jars and decorated pill slabs were made, and these are now among the highlights of many private as well as public collections.

English porcelain during the eighteenth century frequently based its enamelled, as well as its blue-and-white, decoration upon Chinese originals. The French language was used to describe a great deal of Oriental porcelain, mainly because much of the early European literature on the subject was in that

45

language. As a result, many porcelain colours retain their French names: for example, *famille rose, famille verte, famille jaune, famille noire,* to name a few. (These terms are explained in the glossary.)

The Continental porcelain works and potters produced many pieces, particularly vases and figure groups, of outstanding beauty. The English factories were unable to rival such lavish work in the eighteenth century mainly through lack of patronage, whereas the reverse was the case in France and Germany. When we consider that the main English factories were concentrating mainly on table wares rather than figures to ensure the regular sales needed to keep them in business, what they did achieve appears so much the greater. It must be acknowledged that while the soft paste figures may lack the technical brilliance of the German hard paste, the English pieces have a disarming charm.

Yet Continental influence from France and Germany, particularly from the royal manufactories of Meissen and Sèvres, was strongly felt and had a considerable impact on English ceramic art. The style of the Royal Porcelain factory at Sèvres, which removed from Vincennes in 1756, was copied in England with considerable brilliance in the nineteenth century, especially by Minton and Coalport and some fine colours were achieved. Here is a list of some of these colours with their dates of introduction: *bleu de roi* and *gros bleu* in 1749; *bleu turquin* (turquoise) in 1752; *rose Pompadour,* much copied in England and also known as *rose du Barry,* in 1757; and a fine apple green known as *en camaien,* (that is, different shades of the same colour) in 1766. In 1751 the factory introduced *bisque,* that is unglazed and uncoloured, figures. They met with great success, so much so that Derby followed suit, also with highly satisfactory results. The English term for *bisque* is 'biscuit'.

European styles also affected porcelain design, particularly the bases of figures. Attention to style can frequently be of major help in dating porcelain, and a brief mention of the major styles, with which the reader will no doubt already be familiar in other contexts, as they are used in reference to porcelain, will be useful.

The first European style to be seen in porcelain is the BAROQUE. It has good balance, symmetry, and a sense of strength. Figure bases tend to be plain. It was in greatest vogue between the early eighteenth century and 1740. Next came ROCOCO, which is sometimes called 'the spirit of European porcelain'. French in origin, it is full of flourishes and scrolls, rock- and shell-shaped bases, and is usually asymmetrical. At its best it displays a quality of delicate lightness and vigour. The height of its popularity was between 1740 and 1765. A vulgar ROCOCO was also produced in the nineteenth century. A revolt against excessive decoration came in the form of the NEO-CLASSICAL style, which was much influenced by the Roman discoveries at Pompeii and Herculaneum. It lasted from 1760 to the early nineteenth century.

Many Continental potters, decorators and modellers had a direct influence on English pottery and porcelain, for in the nineteenth century many Frenchmen came to work in England. Minton in particular encouraged them to come, although several other factories were also quick to seize upon their skills, a subject dealt with more fully in Chapter 7.

Of all the modellers copied during the eighteenth century, Johann Kändler had most impact. Many English figures are derived from Kändler originals. Kändler, who died in 1775, held the post of Modellmeister at Meissen from 1731. His style was mainly that of the Baroque and his lively versatility made him a leading force in ceramics throughout Europe. Figures from Italian comedy, including the magnificent dancing group of Harlequin and Columbine modelled in 1744, the seasons, the elements and the arts have always been favourites with collectors, and collecting them is a costly pleasure. Kändler also made some fine bird models, many of them observed from nature.

The other name to be remembered with that of Kändler is Johann Bottger (1682-1719). It was Bottger who, while working for the king of Prussia, carried out the successful experiments with porcelain that led to the establishment in 1710 of the Royal Porcelain Manufactory at Meissen and the first hard paste in Europe.

Marks add much to the story of any object, and nineteenth-century marks frequently contain considerable detail for the intelligent interpreter. The extraordinary thing is that so many people, when confronted with a mark, will read its message inaccurately. It is difficult to account for this apart from the fact that surprisingly few individuals are accurate observers and that most people see what they want to see rather than what really confronts them. It is not uncommon for pattern numbers to be mistaken for dates, or for printed dates of a factory's establishment to be considered the date of manufacture. Before listing several important guides to nineteenth-century dating, it is worth reiterating the value of looking closely at earlier specimens of the type being studied. There have been many occasions when well loved objects have been in the possession of families for several generations yet everyone has failed to see the marks. Rare marks on a genuine object are more likely to be discreetly placed than boldly paraded as is the practice with a copy.

Family attributions may also lead to sadly distorted facts and later disappointments. For example, the ownership of a valued object that has been in the possession of several members of a family often results in the lifespans of the people concerned being added together and thereby producing a completely distorted number of years. Thus for example the date believed to be 1750 under these conditions is far more likely to be 1880 in reality. Always regard a generation as being a span of thirty years. Even more difficult to eradicate than the method of family dating mentioned is the attribution of some long dead member of a family who has written an identification of a vase or figure group on a piece of stamp-paper stuck on its base. Firm evidence to the contrary will seldom shake family faith in their stamp-paper heritage. There is of course no harm in this, but it so often leads to great disillusion at a later date.

Here, then, is a list of pointers worth remembering when examining nineteenth-century marks.
1. If the word 'England' forms part of a mark then the date of the object must be after 1891.
2. 'Made in England' or 'Bone China' always indicate twentieth-century manufacture.
3. 'Trade Mark' indicates that the object was produced after the Trade Mark Act of 1862.
4. 'Royal' in a factory mark indicates manufacture since 1850.
5. 'Limited' or 'Ltd.' in a firm's trade name proves a date after 1861.
6. Printed marks that bear the name of a pattern, such as 'Asiatic Pheasant', will always be later than 1810.
7. Printed marks bearing the royal arms are never earlier than the nineteenth century and may well be modern.

Chapter 4

English pottery

Whenever the term 'The Potteries' is used in England it is immediately associated in peoples' minds with the county of Staffordshire. Staffordshire pottery has become renowned throughout the world and the potteries have developed into one of Britain's major industries. The early years of potting in Staffordshire, however, were primitive to say the very least, and could in no way be described in the late seventeenth or early eighteenth centuries as a major industry. For most of the early Staffordshire potters it was a part-time occupation, for their main livelihood came from such occupations as farming and inn-keeping.

The question often arises as to why it should be that with such major deposits of china clay and china stone situated in the south-west of England the potteries should have taken root so firmly in Staffordshire: the answer of course is coal. The discovery of coal at Stoke-on-Trent changed the landscape and was in due course to produce the distinctive feature of the coal-fired bottle ovens, so that by the end of the last century Stoke-

32 Staffordshire pottery cup with 'feathered' and 'combed' slip decoration (left) and mug with 'combed' slip decoration (right). Late seventeenth century. City Museum and Art Gallery, Stoke-on-Trent.

on-Trent had earned the reputation of being one of the dirtiest towns in England. The kilns, with their belching chimneys pouring vast clouds of smoke into the sky, appeared to have placed the potteries under a permanent and unhealthy cloud. Today the bottle ovens still standing may be counted in tens, whereas once they were numbered in thousands.

The advent of gas and electric furnaces again altered the face of Staffordshire and with it the lives of its work-force. Imagine, for example, the great bee-hive shaped brick ovens being laboriously stacked with clay saggers, each packed with ceramic wares of varying kinds. The firing of such an oven was

IRISH SEA

NORTH SEA

·Leeds

·Liverpool

·Rockingham flints

·Chester

salt sand clay

The Potteries ·Derby

Caughley coal lead

felspar ·Coalport

flints

Lowestoft·

· Worcester

BRISTOL
CHANNEL

·Bristol

Chelsea
Bow

flints

Bideford

ball clay

ball clay

flints

ball clay

Cornish stone

china clay

Teignmouth

steatite Plymouth

ENGLISH CHANNEL

Map showing the main
centres of pottery
manufacture, sources of raw
materials, and harbours
used.

supervised by the fireman whose skill was required to create
the correct temperatures, temperatures at which the inside of
the base of these double-walled structures would become
white hot. Large quantities of beer were consumed by the men
responsible for the fires and finally, as the oven cooled, came
the hazardous task of removing the saggers. In order to save
time and money men would enter the kilns while the heat was
still very considerable, wearing sacks over their heads and
shoulders while others doused them with water. Such, for
many, was the way of life in the potteries during the nineteenth
century.

One of the earliest potters of whom note must be taken is

51

John Dwight of Fulham. From medieval times a considerable quantity of German salt-glazed stoneware had been imported into England from the Rhineland. Probably the most well-known examples of this ware are the large 'Bellarmine' jugs, sometimes called 'Greybeards', and known as such because of the bearded caricature masks of the unpopular Cardinal Bellarmine that they bear. (Such jugs still exist in considerable numbers but those which bear no mask and are quite plain are usually English, while rare examples are sometimes found with applied Tudor roses or coats of arms.) Dwight obtained his patent for manufacturing his own stoneware from Charles II, producing domestic wares and also figures which tend to be of a pale buff stoneware and are today much admired rarities. Although educated for the Church and appointed registrar to the Bishop of Chester, Dwight very soon turned his thoughts and skills towards becoming a potter. His pottery was established at Fulham in 1671 and he took out several further patents which resulted in legal proceedings during the 1690s when he sued other potters in Fulham and also in Staffordshire because of patent infringements. His main output consisted of hollow wares thrown on the wheel, including such things as jugs, bowls and mugs.

One of Dwight's finest achievements is the Prince Rupert bust now in the British Museum. Once believed to have been modelled by Grinling Gibbons (1648-1721) because of its quality, it is now thought to be the work of John Bushnell (1619-1682) who was also responsible for a terra cotta bust of Charles II to be seen in the Fitzwilliam Museum, Cambridge. Less elaborate examples of Dwight's own work may be seen at the Victoria and Albert Museum in London.

Dwight's family continued with the pottery after his death

35 *Far left:* Brown salt-glazed stoneware bottle with marbled black and white clay patterning and applied moulded reliefs. John Dwight, *c.* 1690. Victoria and Albert Museum, London.

36 *Centre:* 'Malling jug' with a silver mounted rim. Tin glazed jugs of this type, with their mottled decoration, take their name from West Malling in Kent, where the first example was found. London, 1550-75. Birmingham Museums and Art Gallery.

37 *Above:* Bellarmine salt-glazed bottle. John Dwight, *c.* 1680. Victoria and Albert Museum, London.

38 Salt-glazed stoneware mug with a silver mounted rim. John Dwight, 1682. Victoria and Albert Museum, London.

39 White salt-glazed stoneware figure of Dwight's dead daughter, Lydia. Victoria and Albert Museum, London.

40 Recumbent figure of Lydia Dwight, inscribed 'Lydia Dwight Dyed March 3, 1672'. Possibly modelled by Grinling Gibbons. John Dwight, *c.* 1672. Victoria and Albert Museum, London.

41 *Right:* Dwight salt-glazed stoneware life-size bust of Prince Rupert, *c.* 1680. British Museum, London.

42 *Far right:* A smaller Dwight bust of Charles II. Victoria and Albert Museum, London.

in 1703 but the wares became more coarse and generally rather unsophisticated. Some excellent stonewares were also being manufactured in various other parts of England, most notably at Nottingham and Bristol.

An early form of decorative earthenware which, although rare, has attracted collectors for generations, is known as slipware. The term slip is used to describe a loose clay that has been diluted with water into a creamy mixture. It is usually applied to a brick-coloured clay on which it is trailed, rather in the way that a cake is iced. Wave, trellis and floral designs abound. Particularly valued are items bearing figures, inscriptions, portraits and dates, in other words the documentary piece. Such information always enhances the interest and value of an object.

While slipware was by no means confined to Staffordshire, the most prized examples originated from that county. The most well-known name to be found on slipware is that of Thomas Toft, which occurs on pieces produced between 1680 and 1690. Other members of the Toft family such as James and Ralph, also appear. Further names of note are William Taylor and Ralph Simpson. It is still not known whether the individuals named were themselves potters or whether they were the persons for whom the pottery was made. These slipwares form the first truly English decorative table wares. Important decorations include royal arms and the occasional representation of William III. Most slipware takes the form of plates, chargers and dishes but delightful waisted cups are also found.

Because the decoration on slipware is so simple to apply it was used over a long period, and while slipwares are most highly regarded when they date from the late seventeenth

century it was also produced during the eighteenth and nineteenth centuries by country potters, and continues to attract many potters today. In 1686 Doctor Plot published his *Natural History of Staffordshire* and in it included a description of the original technique of decorating slipware:

'. . . they slip or paint them, with their severall sorts of slip, according as they designe their work; when the first slip is dry, laying on the others at their leisure, the orange slip making the ground, and the white and red; which two colours they break with a wire brush, much after the manner they doe when they marble paper . . .'

Among the other distinctive slipwares are those from Wrotham in Kent, with their popular tyg shape, that is a pottery vessel of beaker shape with a number of applied handles. Other Wrotham-ware shapes are flagons and dishes.

Yet another type of slipware is known as Jackfield. Jackfield is in Shropshire and red clay products glazed with a glossy black slip have traditionally been associated with that area. Excavations have in recent years provided evidence to suggest that it was also made in other parts of Britain, for example Staffordshire. Once again Jackfield pieces are most distinctive and the ware is most often represented by large teapots, some of which bear documentary inscriptions in gold.

Salt-glaze wares, with their special feel and appearance, have proved attractive to generations of collectors. Although the first commercial examples of salt-glaze were not produced

43 An interesting Nottingham double-walled salt-glazed brown stoneware mug. The outer wall has incised and pierced decoration. Inscribed 'Nottn. 1703'.

44 Slip-decorated dish showing the incident when Charles II took refuge in the Boscabel oak tree, *c.* 1675. British Museum, London.

45 A particularly fine slip-decorated earthenware dish with two shades of brown and white. Staffordshire, *c.* 1675. Victoria and Albert Museum, London.

46 Posset pot with slip-trailed floral decoration. The inscription round the rim reads 'The Best is Not To Good For You 1696'. City Museum and Art Gallery, Stoke-on-Trent.

47 The early use of slip decoration was by no means confined to Staffordshire, and this rare tyg was made of a red earthenware at Wrotham in Kent. Victoria and Albert Museum, London.

48 Salt-glazed brown stoneware two-handled bowl, c. 1740. Victoria and Albert Museum, London.

49 *Above:* Large dish depicting 'The Pelican in her Piety', c. 1675. Victoria and Albert Museum, London.

50 *Below:* Rare Wrotham dish with incised or 'sgraffito' decoration, 1699. British Museum, London.

55

in England until the last thirty years of the seventeenth century, the original discovery of the glaze was accidental and was made in Germany. It must have been noticed many years earlier that if salt water was allowed to boil over the side of an earthenware pot for any length of time, a glaze of sorts was the result. Simeon Shaw, who knew so many of the later Staffordshire potters, records in his *History of the Staffordshire Potteries*, published at Hanley in 1829, the discovery of salt-glaze:

'About 1680, the method of GLAZING WITH SALT, was suggested by an accident; we give the names of the parties as delivered down by tradition. In this as in many other improvements in Pottery, a close investigation of one subject has frequently reflected fresh light upon another; something altogether unexpected has been presented to notice; and not infrequently from an accident comparatively trivial has resulted a discovery of paramount importance. At Stanley Farm, (a short mile from the small Pottery of Mr. Palmer, at Bagnall, five miles East of Burslem) the servant of Mr. Joseph Yates, was boiling in an earthen vessel, a strong lixivium of common salt, to be used some way in curing pork; but during her temporary absence, the liquor effervesced, and some ran over the sides of the vessel, quickly causing them to become red hot; the muriatic acid decomposed the surface and when cold, the sides were partially glazed. Mr. Palmer availed himself of the hint thus obtained, and commenced making a fresh sort—the common BROWN WARE of our day; and was soon followed by the manufacturers in Holden Lane, Green Head, and Brown Hills; the proximity of their situation to the Salt-Wyches, affording great facility for procuring the quantity of Salt required for their purposes.'

It is a nice story but it really does no more than highlight something that must have been observed long before. It is thought that a highly-skilled Dutch potter named John Phillip Elers was among the first to appreciate the chemical changes that were involved in this kind of glaze. It was used increasingly during the eighteenth century and it may be useful to have a brief description of how such objects were fired. Kilns were made with carefully prepared apertures through which common salt (sodium chloride) could be thrown towards the end of the firing period. In the immense heat the salt would become volatile and rise around the objects in the kiln in a great cloud of white vapour. This would react to the water vapour in the kiln and two chemical changes would then take place. The hydrogen in the water would mingle with the chlorine of the

51 White salt-glazed mug depicting the naval victory of Admiral Vernon at Portobello in 1739. Victoria and Albert Museum, London.

52 Elers unglazed red stoneware mug with applied moulded decoration. Victoria and Albert Museum, London.

53 Fine red stoneware coffee pot of the type made by Elers. Late seventeenth or early eighteenth century. City Museum and Art Gallery, Stoke-on-Trent.

54 Elers mug clearly showing the outline of a stamped decoration. City Museum and Art Gallery, Stoke-on-Trent.

salt and become hydrochloric acid. In turn, the oxygen and the sodium would form a silicate. It was this film of silicate that glazed the wares distributed in the kiln. Once handled, salt-glaze is unmistakeable as it has a curious granular texture, rather like orange peel.

It is not only for his work in salt-glaze that John Elers will be remembered, as a very hard and fine red ware was produced by him and is usually referred to as Elersware. He had come to this country from Holland with his brother David around the time of William of Orange, and had settled in Staffordshire a few miles from Burslem where he found a clay which was ideal for the manufacture of red stoneware. It is believed that John Elers was largely responsible for the pottery while David handled the administration of their business. The fine, high-quality clay which formed the body of the red ware allowed it to be lathe-turned before firing and these highly finished pieces became extremely popular. They also used an interesting form of decoration: applying pieces of damp clay to the lathe-turned article and stamping it with a geometrical, floral or sprig pattern. The superfluous clay was then very carefully cut away.

It is said that the Elers brothers maintained the greatest secrecy over the mixing of their clays. They had established their pottery at Bradwell, north of Newcastle-under-Lyme, in the 1690s, and it was there that they evolved a classic method for the purification of clay. By suspending their clays in water all coarser particles sank to the bottom while the remainder were drawn off into pans where the water would evaporate in the sun. The obvious drawback to this refining method was that it was dependent upon good weather and prevented year-round working. A more commercial process was invented by Ralph Shaw of Burslem in 1732 when he devised the drying of clay on shallow kilns heated by flues beneath.

The variety and shape of the Elers red wares were largely inspired by the increasing demand for tea in England and the importing of red stonewares from Yi-hsing, the Chinese potteries west of the great lake in Kiangsu. These were to be the models for the first European teapots made by Dwight and Elers. During the nineteenth century many copies were made of the early Elersware and care therefore needs to be exercised when confronted with such pieces. The Elers brothers also made a black earthenware known as 'Egyptian black'. This was later to be improved by Josiah Wedgwood into the celebrated black basalt.

John Astbury is another potter of importance in the early

eighteenth century. He worked mainly with earthenware and legend has it that he acquired many of the Elers brothers' manufacturing secrets by obtaining employment with them by posing as a half-wit—the Elers brothers are believed to have employed such men in order to prevent intelligent outside discussion of their work. So industrial espionage has been with us for a very long time!

Astbury became deeply interested in the nature of the clays being used. As we have already seen, while other parts of Britain also had excellent clay deposits, these existed in greater variety in Staffordshire and were supported by the availability of easily mined long-flame bituminous coal. The geological excellence of Staffordshire was further increased by the discovery in 1670 of rock salt near Northwich, in neighbouring Cheshire, and the mining of lead ore in Derbyshire.

Pipe clays, so-called because they were used for the manufacture of clay tobacco pipes, were found in thin seams. From about 1720 similar clays were imported from Devon and Dorset. These became known as ball clays because they were dug out in 35 lb (15·8 kg) balls with a tool not unlike an adze. The clay was then carried by sea from the ports of Bideford, Teignmouth and Wareham to be unloaded at the port of Chester and from there carried by pack-horse into north Staffordshire. John Astbury was delighted with the ball clays and he was also quick to see the importance of adding ground flint into his pottery body to make it harder and smoother. Other potters had also used flint a few years earlier and many

55 Chinese Yi-hsing red stoneware teapot with relief decoration, a kind that probably influenced the work of the Elers brothers and other Staffordshire potters. Victoria and Albert Museum, London.

56 Whieldon coffee pot with crabstock handle. Victoria and Albert Museum, London.

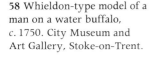

57 Figure of a Turk. Whieldon, *c.* 1750. Victoria and Albert Museum, London.

58 Whieldon-type model of a man on a water buffalo, *c.* 1750. City Museum and Art Gallery, Stoke-on-Trent.

workers died of pneumoconiosis when working in the thick dust of the dry stamp mills, where the flint was ground down. In 1726 a patent was taken out for the grinding of flints in water which eliminated many of the earlier problems. The potteries were now beginning to grow and as local skills increased all that remained was the necessity of providing better transport facilities by road and by water, and it was not long before all of these hopes were fulfilled.

The charming Astbury figures of brown and white clays under a transparent lead glaze are easily recognised; their blackcurrant eyes and naive modelling are their hallmarks. Similar figures which are lead-glazed but stained with metallic oxides are referred to as Astbury Whieldon, while earthenware figures with stained or tortoiseshell glazes are known as Whieldon. This classification helps to define the three types of early figures but there must have been many other potters in Staffordshire working in a similar fashion to those already named.

Thomas Whieldon is among the most revered of the early Staffordshire potters, the last of a long line of peasant craftsmen, but while his trade was considerable he firmly belonged to that highly individual period just prior to the new age of industrialisation. He made toys and chimney ornaments of all kinds and his figure models of birds and animals are especially delightful. The birds usually have a variegated glaze, while the small animals, particularly the cats, were made of agate ware which imitated agate stone by the layering of different col-

oured clays before cutting and moulding into shape, or by the use of differently coloured slips on the surface of the figure. When made of solid colour clays, such wares are called solid agate and when surface colouring is applied they are known as surface colouring agate. An outline of Whieldon's life and something of an insight into his character is once again given us by Simeon Shaw:

'In 1740 Mr. Thomas Whieldon's manufactory at Little Fenton consisted of a small range of low buildings, all thatched. His early productions were knife hafts, for the Sheffield cutlers; and Snuff Boxes, for the Birmingham Hardwaremen, to finish with hoops, hinges and springs; which he himself usually carried in a basket to the tradesmen; and being much like agate, they were greatly in request. He also made toys and chimney ornaments, coloured in either the clay state or bisquet, by zaffre, manganese, copper, etc., and glazed with black, red, or white lead. He also made black glazed tea and coffee pots. Tortoise-shell and melon table plates, (with ornamented edge, and six scollopes, as in the specimens kept by Andrew Boon, of the Honeywall Stoke) and other useful articles. Mr. A. Wood made models and moulds of these articles also pickle leaves, crab stock handles and cabbage leave spouts, for tea and coffee pots, all which utensils, with candlesticks, chocolate cups, and tea ware, were much improved, and his connections extended subsequently, when Mr. J. Wedgwood became his managing partner. He was a shrewd and careful person. To prevent his productions being imitated in quality or shape, he always buried the broken articles; and a few months ago, we witnessed the unexpected exposure of some of these, by some miners attempting to get marl in the road at Little Fenton. The fortune he acquired by his industry enabled him to erect a very elegant mansion, near Stoke; where he long enjoyed in the bosom of his family, the fruits of his early economy. He was also Sheriff of the County, in the 26th year of the late reign. The benevolence of his disposition, and his integrity, are honourable traits of character, far superior to the boast of ancestry without personal merit. He died in 1798, at a very old age and in 1828 his relict was interred beside him in Stoke Church yard.'

(It has since been proved that Whieldon died in 1795, three years earlier than stated by Shaw.)

The reference to what are known as crab stock handles is particularly interesting for it was a handle in regular use in Staffordshire pottery between 1740 and 1770. Even the finials

59 Lead-glazed Astbury
Whieldon earthenware
figure of a cavalryman,
c. 1740. Victoria and Albert
Museum, London.

to lids of teapots tend to be of this shape, which does indeed bear similarity to that of the body of a crab. Many of the salt-glaze teapots and coffee pots of this period are decorated in enamels and are largely inspired by Chinese originals, particularly the *famille rose* palette. Decoration was also incised or applied and the general care and attention given to both shape and colouring was largely due to the competitive pressures from foreign and British porcelains. While Whieldon's work was not subjected to such commercial pressure, his wares were nonetheless colourful, with their splashes of brown, green, yellow and manganese. Such colours are best shown off in Whieldon's moulded plates with their feathered or trellised borders and frequently milled edges. His output of such wares, together with his animal figures, are among the most collectable of the early Staffordshire pottery.

It is clear from Astbury's work that he favoured the development of figure modelling and his rolled pipe clay figures always

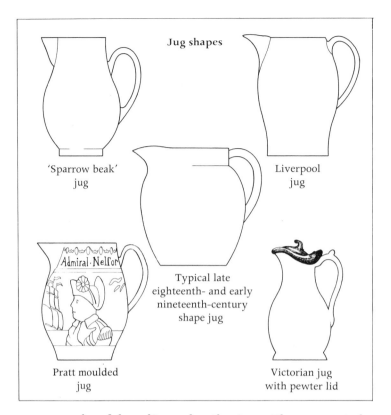

Jug shapes

'Sparrow beak' jug

Liverpool jug

Typical late eighteenth- and early nineteenth-century shape jug

Pratt moulded jug

Admiral·Nelſon

Victorian jug with pewter lid

possess a cheerful quality and enthusiasm. These were to be surpassed, in both quality and beauty, in the second half of the eighteenth century by the astonishing range of figures model- led by the Wood family of Burslem. In the middle of the eighteenth century the use of plaster of Paris moulds was introduced into Staffordshire from France by Ralph Daniel. Plaster moulds were ideal for ease of use, speed and detailed moulding, but the rival method of pressing 'bats' or cakes of clay into a mould was to continue for a long time, causing moulded decoration to become increasingly poor. Today plas- ter of Paris moulds are still regarded as the finest method of production available.

Thus the range of English pottery was being extended by potters like Elers, Astbury and Whieldon who experimented with new techniques. They continued to make salt-glaze, however, and it will be useful at this point, before turning to other wares, to give a break-down of the four main stages of its development:

1. *Before 1720.* Engine-turned vessels with impressed or ap- plied ornament.

2. *1720-1740.* The introduction of flint into the clay enabled crisper, finer work to be produced.

3. *1740-1760.* Popular use of coloured enamels in the decoration of salt-glazed wares.

4. *1760-1780.* Increased use of pierced work and a general decline in production.

The market for salt-glaze was being steadily undermined by the development of creamwares with their simple painted or transfer printed decoration. Creamware will be considered in the next chapter, and let us in the meantime return to other forms of English pottery, notably Staffordshire figures and English Delft.

Staffordshire pottery figures

The demand for pottery ornaments at the beginning of the eighteenth century was not large, mainly because social conditions were not yet ready for it. The Staffordshire chimney ornaments came into their own towards the end of the century, and as the nineteenth century progressed so the demand for such ornaments grew. In other words, with the creation of more urban areas and homes with a 'best room' or 'parlour' where furniture and other objects were displayed, pottery became something of a status symbol. Such pieces differed from the earlier cottage ornaments which tended to portray scenes of sport, work and courtship.

The Astbury figures of salt-glazed stoneware, decorated

60 White salt-glazed 'pew group', *c.* 1730-45. British Museum, London.

with coloured glazes under a final lead glaze, were produced from moulds, with a great deal of hand finishing. Whieldon's application of coloured glazes is haphazard, and the work of both men may easily be criticised on many counts if precision of detail is regarded as paramount. Yet for many collectors the soldiers, pew groups, musicians and horsemen of this period possess all the charm in the world. Perhaps the attraction is due to the humble materials used and the spontaneous, child-like approach of the modellers. The majority of such figures possess humour and an apparently insatiable concern for such trimmings of dress as buttons, bows, buckles and curled wigs.

The pottery figures that followed were the work of potters who had clearly come of age in the process; something of the earlier imaginative exuberance was lost, but it was replaced with a high level of sophistication. The potters largely responsible for this change were the Wood family of Burslem.

Ralph Wood senior (1715-1772) had worked for John Astbury and Thomas Whieldon before starting to manufacture pottery on his own account in Burslem in about 1754. He was responsible for some superb and justly famous figures, plaques and Toby jugs. Many of the pieces made by this family can be identified with certainty because they impressed many of their figures with mould numbers. Also to be found are the marks of the firm – R. WOOD or *Ra Wood* or *Ra Wood, Burslem* – which are believed to be the marks of father and son. A very rare rebus in the form of a group of trees impressed in the side of a base is also thought to be a mark of Ralph Wood senior.

It would be perhaps better to identify the work of the Woods by their quality. Ralph Wood senior is distinguished by the splendid modelling of his figures and the superbly lustrous transparent glazes that he employed. There was no slipping or dabbing of glazes and trusting to good fortune: care had become the watchword and Ralph Wood applied his coloured glazes with a brush exactly where they were required. To obtain flesh tints he used a highly unusual pale manganese purple.

Similar colouring techniques were also used by Ralph Wood junior (1748-1795) but he went on to adopt the use of enamel colours, as did his cousin Enoch Wood (1759-1840). This new method of decoration by the use of overglaze enamels was very open to misuse and could be applied with a garish brashness like a woman who has failed to understand make-up. Enoch Wood was the son of Aaron Wood (1717-1785), who was the brother of Ralph Wood senior and a brilliant modeller and mould maker. So many of the potters' skills seem inherent in

61 Pottery figure of a young girl decorated in a coloured translucent glaze. The impressed mark reads 'R. Wood' Burslem. *C.* 1770. Victoria and Albert Museum, London.

this family that it is little wonder that the portrait busts by Enoch Wood should be outstanding. Enoch and Ralph Wood junior worked in partnership until Ralph's early death in 1795 when Enoch Wood joined James Caldwell. In 1819 Caldwell was bought out by Enoch Wood and the business then became known as Enoch Wood and Sons. As the father of twelve children 'and Sons' was more than usually appropriate!

The portrait bust of John Wesley is probably the finest work by Enoch Wood but his use of bright enamel colours and his misuse of silver lustre has somewhat undermined his reputation as a potter. As a man he was held in highest esteem in the potteries, and was chief constable of Burslem for two years. Enoch Wood was among the first real collectors of Staffordshire pottery and with his family background and associations he must have owned pieces of the greatest importance. Unfortunately no inventory or catalogue was ever made and when he died in 1840 the collection was dispersed.

Great collections were made in the nineteenth century and the finest private collection of that period which I have seen is that formed by Henry Willett of Brighton, now in the Brighton Museum and Art Gallery. In 1899 it was lent to the Bethnal Green Museum, a branch of the Victoria and Albert Museum, and a most useful catalogue was produced, although unfortunately copies are now difficult to obtain. The catalogue lists 1,715 objects and it is possible to sense the pleasure that Henry Willett must have enjoyed while gathering them together. His brief introduction to the catalogue is well worth quoting for it demonstrates so well the very best of motives for collecting anything:

'This collection has been formed with a view to develop the idea that the history of the country may to a large extent be traced on its homely pottery, and it is not to be regarded as an exhibition of ceramic art.

'On the mantelpieces of many cottage homes may be found representations which the inmates admire and revere, as their ancestors have done before them. They form, in fact, a kind of unconscious survival of the Lares and Penates of the Ancients.

'The classification, whilst confessedly arbitrary, has been made not so much in reference to the maker, the time and place of manufacture, but rather with regard to the greater human interest which each object presents.

'June, 1899.   HENRY WILLETT.'

Willett then goes on to explain his reference to Lares and Penates:

'The Lares and Penates were household gods of the Romans. The former were grouped into various classes, such as: *lares domestici*, departed spirits of the household, only good men being thus honoured; *lares publici*, benefactors to the nation; *lares marini*, victors in naval battles and others. There were also public and private penates, protectors and promoters of happiness and concord. Every meal was a kind of sacrifice to them, often ending in a libation.'

The catalogue's contents list will also help to provide the new collector with an idea of the variety of interest covered in such pottery: Royalty and Loyalty, Military Heroes, Naval Heroes, Soldiers and Sailors, England and France, England and America, Statesmen, Clubs and Societies, Philanthropy, Crime, Professions and Trades, Architecture, Scripture, Religion, Music, Drama, Poetry, Science and Literature, Sporting, Field Sports, Pastimes and Amusements, Agriculture, Conviviality and Teetotalism, Domestic Incidents.

The Wood family modelled a great range of figures of rustic inspiration, from birds nesting to larger animals such as lions and elephants. The seasons were represented, as were many classical figures and a number of literary and scientific personalities such as Milton, Chaucer, Pope and Newton. Some of the Ralph Wood figures were modelled by the Frenchman John Voyez.

An active potter during the early years of the nineteenth century with a considerable output in the field of figures and toys was a man named John Walton (working *c.*1806-1850). He tended to like somewhat sentimental subjects such as allegori-

62 *Far left:* A rare 'Fair Hebe' jug, one of the originals modelled by the Frenchman Jean Voyez, and signed and dated 1788. Voyez worked for numerous Staffordshire potters and some of his jugs have been attributed to the Wood family. Those decorated in enamel colours will be later versions. Hebe was the Greek goddess of youth. Victoria and Albert Museum, London.

63 *Above:* Figure of a gardener. Walton, Burslem, 1825. Victoria and Albert Museum, London.

WALTON

Impressed mark, found on backs of bocage figures, *c.* 1818-35

cal representations of Hope and Charity. His modelling was straightforward and he made great use of the bocage, which is modelled leaves and flowers forming a background, and support for the figures. Soft paste figures needed such support in the kiln and the bocage made a decorative virtue of necessity.

It is thought that the bocage originated on the Continent where figures in stage productions were observed in front of moveable scenery in the form of trees; the idea was then tried out in porcelain and later its use became widespread. Walton's work is often marked on the back of the model in relief-moulded capitals or impressed on a scroll.

Other potters are associated with Walton because of a similarity in style. Most important among these is Ralph Salt (1792-1846): his mark is impressed.

Some very interesting religious figures were manufactured by this school. A famous model is that of the tithe pig. Here we find a man with a pig, a parson, a woman with a child, some piglets, eggs and sheaves of corn. Behind the figures is a bocage. The tithe is due but the wife is offering the parson her baby instead of the expected pig!

James Neale, a London merchant, met the potter, Humphrey Palmer, and took over his business at the Church Works, Hanley, in 1776. His late eighteenth-century wares were well chosen and in the best of taste. His work is recognised not only by the good potting but also by his frequent use of rectangular or square bases around which a red line has often been painted. The business closed soon after 1814 when Neale died. Neale's small figures of the seasons are considered superior to those of Ralph Wood junior.

At the same time, around 1775, a particular type of lead-glazed earthenware was being made at Lane Delph by William Pratt. The ware, primarily jugs and figure models, had a lightweight body, often white but sometimes tinged with blue, and the colours that were used in decoration are browns, greens, yellow, black and orange.

The factory was taken over in 1810 by William Pratt's son Felix and in the nineteenth century it was this factory that produced pot lids. However, it is only the pottery and palette originally used that is termed Prattware.

The work of Obadiah Sherratt (b. 1755), who worked at Hot Lane, Burslem, was continued after his death by his second wife, Martha, until about 1860. While so much of the Staffordshire pottery output was handled in a light and somewhat bucolic manner, the Sherratt figures are bluntly to the point in their vigorous portrayal of life about them and of news stories

SALT

Impressed mark, c. 1820-46

Rare impressed or moulded mark, c. 1776-86

Neale & Wilson

Impressed, c. 1784-95

of the day. Certainly crude versions of classical figures were attempted, probably copied from Derby originals, but they are not the pieces for which Sherratt is remembered and collected.

Sherratt groups include 'The Death of Monrow' [sic] which depicts the fate of Lieutenant Hector Monroe who was killed and carried off by a tiger near Calcutta. Some rare examples of this group show the tiger as being black rather than striped. Temperance campaigns were assisted by his morality groups, one of which carries the title 'Teetotal Bench'. In this instance accurate dating is assisted by the fact that the word teetotal was not coined until 1833.

Maria Martin and the murder in the Red Barn of 1828 are portrayed, as is bull-baiting. This, his most famous group, is so vigorous that it exudes the cruelty of a sport which Sherratt would certainly have known at first-hand. Bull-baiting was made illegal in 1835, but in Staffordshire it was continued for as long as possible. Suddenly we discover that the English countryside was not all quaint shepherds and shepherdesses, and that life was also riddled with ignorance and barbarity. In an issue of the *Staffordshire Advertiser* in November 1833 is this

65 Fine lead-glazed Staffordshire figure group depicting 'Bacchus and Ariadni', c. 1790. Fitzwilliam Museum, Cambridge.

dreadful account which enables us to see the pottery of Sherratt as social document:

'At Rowley Regis wake a two-year-old bull was worried in the most brutal manner. Either on the Monday or Tuesday one of the bull's horns was broken off, and the following day the other shared the same fate, and a portion of the tongue was also torn out of its mouth by one of the dogs. On the Thursday he was again dragged to the stake and worried for hours, the whole of his head and face being mangled and covered in blood, in a manner too shocking to describe. Two iron horns had also been riveted on to the stumps, and the bellowings and groans of the wretched beast, while undergoing this barbarous operation, are said to have been truly appaling [sic].'

There are differences to be observed among the bull-baiting groups. Some show the bull with dogs and a man standing at its side, some with a man under the bull and some combine all these features.

Sherratt's large model of 'Polito's Menagerie' is most ambitious, with its human and animal figures. Sherratt also had an eye for marital conflict as a group called 'Battle for the Breeches' well illustrates. In the Willett collection catalogue mentioned earlier, there is an earthenware mug that depicts 'Peggy Plumper proving her man before marriage' or 'Who wears ye breeches'. The mug also bears an inscription in verse that has little to commend it apart from the humour of its times, humour which, no doubt, explains the popularity of such examples with collectors today.

Peggy Plumper, a lass well made tall and pretty,
Was courted by sweet Sammy Spar of ye city:
They jog'd on in courtship, Sam would have gone faster,
But Peg w'd not Wed, till she knew who was Master.

Tho' says She we may live and ne'er quarrel for riches,
Yet it may not be so, about wearing the Breeches.
So saying she squar'd up to Sam very clever,
Thinks he for to gain her the time's now or never.

They had several rounds, who'd the best none did know, Sir,
At last Sam gave Peg a fair knock down blow, Sir;
Then he led her to church as loving as could be,
And the Breeches remain'd in ye place where they should be.

The flat pottery table bases of his groups were usually mounted on four or six short legs. A good general rule of thumb when examining old pottery is to remember that the majority of figures made before 1800 have hollow bases, while those made after this date are solid. Lose no opportunity of handling pottery of all kinds whenever a sale or similar occasion arises.

The most well-known form of Staffordshire pottery must surely be the Toby jug: jugs in human form, with the figure usually holding a foaming tankard and a churchwarden pipe. The Toby's hat or lid, usually missing from old examples, formed the cup to drink from. While the production of Toby jugs was not confined to any one manufacturer, they are most frequently associated with the work of Ralph Wood senior and his son Ralph Wood junior. Again it was the coloured translucent glazes that have made the Wood Toby jugs so desirable. The great collector of Toby jugs, Lord Mackintosh, likened such glazes to the light through stained glass windows.

Uncle Toby in Sterne's *Tristram Shandy* and Sir Toby Belch in *Twelfth Night* have both been claimed as the inspiration for the Toby jug, but it is far more likely that the character originated from a print published in London early in the 1760s from the printshop of Carrington and Bowles. The print was the work of Robert Dighton and it was accompanied by a song called 'The Brown Jug'. In the Copeland Spode Museum there is a relief mould that copies the Dighton print but the jugs themselves bear only a passing likeness. I like to think that the jugs were based on a Yorkshireman named Harry Elwes who is said to have received the nickname of Toby Fillpot for having drunk two thousand gallons of ale from a brown jug. More likely Ralph Wood senior simply copied some local real-life character.

Whatever Toby's identity the jugs have created ample fuel for collectors for they have many variations, including such characters as 'Hearty Good Fellow', 'Toby Fillpot', 'Sir Toby Belch', 'The Squire', 'Drunken Parson', 'The Fiddler', 'Admiral Lord Howe', 'Martha Gunn', 'Admiral Jarvis', 'Nightwatchman', 'American Sailor', and so on. The cult of the Toby jug appears to be very much an on-going tradition, and a fine Toby of Winston Churchill was modelled by Leonard Jarvis and decorated with glazes in the Ralph Wood style just after the Second World War. Churchill also appears as a Toby rather earlier, when he formed one of a series modelled by Carruthers Gould for the Royal Stafford Pottery during the First World War. The characters depicted heroes of the day—King George V, Lord Kitchener, Earl Haig, Admiral Beatty and Sir John French. Most of these Tobys were issued in limited editions of a few hundred and are now very definitely collectors' pieces.

66 Pair of Victorian 'flatback' chimney ornaments depicting the Duke and Duchess of Cambridge.

Victorian Staffordshire figures were mentioned in Chapter 1. They are characterised by their 'flatback' form which, as the name indicates, means that they have no modelling on the back. Flatbacks were made in press moulds and date from shortly before the middle of the nineteenth century. They covered a great variety of subjects and many of them were made by Sampson Smith of Longton after 1855. This style of figure could not have been better suited to the mantelpiece and in recent years there has been a complete renewal of interest in them. Figures bearing the name of the character depicted are particularly valued, and many of them are American. Because of demand there has been an influx of reproductions in recent years that have been made from the old moulds. It is a knowledgeable eye that separates the original from the copy, but copies are most frequently detected by their differences in colouring. For example, bases with a brown and green mottled effect should be regarded with suspicion, as copies were made from moulds discovered just after the Second World War until 1962. It is curious that while this type of pottery has risen considerably in value, Toby jugs have not appreciated to anything like the same extent.

English Delft

A class of English pottery that can still be obtained without too much difficulty is English Delft, manufactured in England from the late sixteenth century until about 1800. This ware and the story of its development has already been mentioned in Chapter 3. The earliest name for tin-glazed wares was 'gally-ware' and the makers were known as 'gally potters'. The tin oxide with its hard white surface provided an ideal basis for decoration and tin was easily obtained in this country from the Cornish mines; in fact the Cornish tin mines supplied the raw materials for much of the production of Dutch Delft and Italian Maiolica. Blue and white decoration is very common on English Delft, the various shades of blue being obtained from cobalt. Other colourings were soon in demand for ornamentation: purple and ranges of that colour were derived from manganese, red from iron, green from copper, yellow from antimony. All these colours vary in tone, and after 1700 greater varieties of green, in particular, were developed.

67 Blue-dash portrait dish painted in blue, green, yellow and red. Note the sponged foliage. Brislington, early eighteenth century. The fragment at the side was excavated in Brislington in 1914. City Art Gallery, Bristol.

The first Delftwares made in England were produced by Dutch potters in London and it is difficult to separate the early English products from those made in Holland. From the late 1620s we begin to see Delftware that is definitely English. Some of these pieces bear inscriptions and dates, while blue and white decoration is based on Ming porcelain.

Much of the London output was manufactured at Southwark and in 1969 I obtained a number of fragments of this early Delft from a site between Southwark Cathedral and the Thames. The pottery body is light buff in colour with the tin glaze of eggshell thickness. Foot-rims among the fragments are un-glazed and specimens from one kiln site not only showed a variation in the glaze from a pinkish white to a hard whitish blue, but also demonstrated the variance in the blue tones of the painted decoration itself. Unfortunately this merely under-lines how difficult it frequently is to attribute particular objects to particular factories. However, fine pieces of English Delft may still be obtained far more cheaply than most English porcelains, and as more excavation and research is carried out in the years to come much more information will become available on both the larger and the lesser known factories. In the following pages, I shall discuss in more detail certain types of these wares which are of special interest to the collector.

Delftware was particularly popular for chargers, a type of large circular dish, of which there are four main types: the blue-dash, the portrait, the Adam and Eve, and the tulip. While most English pottery was made for every-day use, blue-dash chargers were mainly produced as ornaments, to be hung on the wall or displayed on court cupboards. They vary in size,

68 *Above:* Polychrome dish with a tulip design. All elements in the design appear to spring from a central source – an indication of Islamic influence. Probably Lambeth, *c.* 1690. Nottingham Castle Museum.

69 *Right:* Polychrome Adam and Eve dish. Lambeth, *c.* 1690. Birmingham Museums and Art Gallery.

the largest being about 16 inches (406 mm). They get their name from the blue dashes painted around their borders. Early pieces are clearly inspired in their decoration by Italian Maiolica as well as Chinese patterns. Of special interest are the blue-dash chargers that also carry royal portraits, the very best being the portraits of William and Mary, either standing together or on their own.

A number of fine examples of portrait chargers exist including ones depicting the English kings Charles I and Charles II. My own personal favourite portrait charger depicts General Monch on horseback. The broad border patterns derive their style from the Chinese blue-and-white dishes of the Kang H'si. Foliage that may appear on chargers of this kind is frequently applied with a sponge and the rather crude splodgy appearance, in contrast to the finer, neater decoration applied with a brush, makes it easily identifiable as such.

Adam and Eve chargers are as their name would suggest, with prominence sometimes being given to the apple and sometimes to the snake. The earliest known example is dated 1635. The sponged foliage mentioned above only appears on late seventeenth-century examples.

Tulip chargers are frequently found with blue dash borders

and their decoration drew much inspiration from Islamic sources: the leaves and stems spring from one central point to radiate over the whole face of the charger.

The painting of all these subjects is invariably crude, partly due no doubt to the cheapness of the ware, yet at the same time most English Delftware has a sense of spontaneity that is truly refreshing. Often a decorator will capture some current event, such as a balloon ascent, and work of this kind adds further to the interest. There are also many curiosities to be found in the form of ointment pots, jars for wet and dry drugs, tiles, pill slabs, shaving bowls, bleeding bowls, posset pots, fuddling cups, trinket pots, flower bricks, tea caddies, candlesticks and cups of all kinds—to say nothing of the mass of plates, teapots, coffee pots, puzzle jugs, punch bowls and so much else. Many of these pieces bear inscriptions that are well worth noting. An old Bristol punch bowl carries a verse typical of West Country humour:

70 Bowl showing Lunardi's balloon ascent at Lambeth in 1783. Lambeth, c. 1783-90. Nottingham Castle Museum.

71 Blue painted barber's bowl, probably Bristol, late seventeenth century. Smaller versions of this bowl (which is $10\frac{1}{4}$ inches (260 mm) in diameter) were also used occasionally as bleeding bowls. Victoria and Albert Museum, London.

> *John Udy of Luxillion his tin was so fine*
> *It gliddered this punch bowl and made it to shine*
> *Pray fill it with punch*
> *Let the tinners sit round*
> *They never will budge till the*
> *Bottom they sound.*
>
> *1731*

Udy is a Cornish name and Luxillion is a parish a few miles from Lostwithiel. The word gliddered is from an old verb meaning to glaze.

The most celebrated inscribed Delft of all are the plates known as the 'Merry Man' plates made at Lambeth. Several such sets were produced, consisting of six plates each bearing a phrase of a complete poem. Lambeth produced an eight-plate set of octagonal blue-and-white decorated plates and further sets of circular plates were made by them later in the seventeenth century and at various periods during the early eighteenth century. The complete verse is as follows:

> *What is a merry man*
> *Let him do what he can*
> *To entertain his guests*
> *With wine and merry jests*
> *But if his wife doth frown*
> *All merriment goes down.*

72 *Above:* Wine bottle with name painted in blue. Height 7¼ inches (184 mm). London, 1651. Royal Scottish Museum, Edinburgh.

73 *Right:* Rare documentary jug painted in blue and purple. Among the many decorative motifs is an applied relief of King David playing his harp. Fitzwilliam Museum, Cambridge.

The spelling used in this verse varies considerably with date and artist; dated examples exist between 1648 and 1742 and only one complete set is at present known.

Lambeth sack bottles, between 6 and 8 inches (152 and 203 mm) high and dating from the middle of the seventeenth century, are also most attractive to collectors, particularly dated examples; while those painted with portraits of Charles II have a special commemorative interest. Many such pieces have a fine white glaze typical of early Lambeth work but there are others with a considerable pinkish tinge giving a somewhat soft appearance.

Successful attributions of eighteenth-century examples are not easy and it is unlikely that the wares of individual potteries in the same area will be separately identified. One of the drawbacks in identification is the fact that many of the potters and decorators frequently moved from pottery to pottery and considerable uniformity was thus brought about in both shape and decoration.

Much Bristol Delftware does incline towards a lavender hue, particularly when decorated with *bianco-sopra-bianco* or white on white. This type of decoration was first used at Faenza in

74 Blue painted plate.
Diameter 9 inches
(228·6 mm). Bristol, 1760.
Victoria and Albert Museum,
London.

Italy during the sixteenth century and it was from that town that the term faience was derived. In their turn the spiral white enamel designs of *bianco-sopra-bianco* were originally taken from Chinese border patterns.

Both Bristol and Liverpool favoured the use of ship decoration, as might be expected, but it tends to occur rather more frequently on Liverpool examples. Liverpool was the only user of transfer prints taken from copper plates which were then used on the Delft tiles.

Rectangular Delft bricks with pierced tops appear to be unique to English Delft. These 'bricks' are usually called flower bricks but in the opinion of some authorities they may have been bulb pots or quill and inkpot holders. Many are decorated in blue and white and were made at Lambeth, Bristol and Liverpool. Where polychrome decoration is used, however, it can be observed that the reds and yellows of Bristol tend to stand proud of the glaze, particularly the reds. Manganese grounds were also used by the main Delftware centres but most of them are usually attributed to manufactories in the West Country.

A polychrome decoration long assumed to have come from Liverpool is formed from a palette which consists of purple,

75 Plate with pale blue glaze. The border is decorated in bianco-sopra-bianco. Probably Bristol, *c.* 1760-70. Merseyside County Museums, Liverpool.

76 *Below:* Fine documentary punch bowl decorated in blue, red and yellow, and showing the 'vessel Whitby'. Liverpool, 1772. Merseyside County Museums, Liverpool.

77 *Far right:* Plate with powdered purple ground. Wincanton or Bristol, 1739. City Art Gallery, Bristol.

blue, green, yellow and red. It is known popularly as 'Fazackerly' since a mug of this decoration is said to have been presented to a Liverpool potter named Thomas Fazackerly. Further pieces decorated in this palette have been excavated in Liverpool, but it would be dangerous to assume that all such examples came from Merseyside.

A decoration that produced rather curious elongated figures of women was the Long Eliza pattern. The name comes from the Dutch Lange Lijzen, the term used for such decorations on Dutch Delftware of the previous century.

Anyone developing a serious interest in Delftware will do well to study the principal literature on the subject and a title is suggested in the bibliography at the end of this volume. He would also be well advised to find out more about the major Delftware centres, and if at all possible, to visit them.

London. Delftware was produced in Aldgate, Lambeth and Southwark, although all London Delftware still tends to be labelled Lambeth. Aldgate began production in the late sixteenth century, while Southwark was once the pottery of Christian Wilhelm who in 1628 was describing himself as 'gallipot maker' to the king.

Bristol. Always a major pottery centre, Bristol contained four Delftware potteries, but Delft was first made just outside the city at Brislington early in the seventeenth century.

In the city itself potteries were established at Temple Back, Limekiln Lane, Avon Street, and in the most celebrated pottery area of the city—Redcliffe Backs.

Wincanton. This Somerset pottery produced Delft during the first half of the eighteenth century. Individual pieces marked Wincanton have been found and manganese borders are also associated with this pottery.

Liverpool. This is another ceramic area of great importance where much else besides Delft was manufactured. In fact several of the Liverpool potters were also making porcelain. The main potteries were:

Richard Holt in Lord Street. Early in the eighteenth century potters came here from Southbank.

Samuel Gilbody in Shaws Brow. Shaws Brow was the main pottery centre of the city, and the Liverpool museums with their fine ceramic collections now stand on the site. Gilbody began early in the eighteenth century. This factory also made porcelain.

Alderman Shaw off Dale Street. Early eighteenth century.

Richard Chaffers on Shaws Brow. Mid eighteenth century. He also made porcelain.

Philip Christian. Mid eighteenth century. He also made porcelain, and took over Chaffers' factory in 1765.

Other Liverpool Delftware potters include George Drinkwater, Zachariah Barnes and James Gibson. Several others can be identified by name if not by their productions.

Lustre

Very little lustre ware is marked and most potteries produced it, so it is often very difficult to attribute to a particular factory.

78 Sunderland lustre plaque. Nineteenth century.

Although lustrous effects had been achieved at a much earlier date, the first lustre patent was not granted until 1810, when Peter Walburton of New Hall patented his 'newly invented method of decorating china, porcelain, earthenware and glass, with gold, silver, platinum, or other metals fluxed with lead, which invention leaves the metals, after being burnt in their metallic state'. Lustre may be divided into the following five categories:

1. The total surface of an object is covered with lustre in order to produce a metallic effect.
2. Lustre is used to heighten relief decoration. This is known as relief lustre.
3. Bands or collars (raised circular bands) of lustre are used in conjunction with painted or transfer decoration.
4. Painted or splashed lustre.
5. Resist lustre.

The most common form of lustre is that made by Dixon Austin & Co. at Sunderland between around 1800 and 1850. These products are usually decorated with transfer prints which may depict the famous Iron Bridge over the river Wear, but a mariner's compass is also frequently seen. These transfer prints are surrounded with irregular splashes of pink lustre. It is most likely that such wares were also introduced at other potteries.

All of these lustres have metallic origins, some of which are confusing. Silver lustre for example is in reality created from platinum salts, and the lustre is so called because of the silver colour that emerges during the firing. Copper lustre is the most common and is derived from copper as the name would suggest. The rare lustres are those known as resist, and are the ones where the decoration on the object is the same colour as the body of the object but stand out from a different coloured lustre ground. There were various methods by which this effect was achieved, the most common being the application of a varnish or wax by stencil, which would 'resist' the lustre when dipped and burned out as the original body when fired. The resist lustres frequently depicting birds or sporting subjects are often quite beautiful and for this reason they are much collected and therefore far more costly than the Sunderland or copper lustres.

When handling lustre wares you will notice that the later Victorian products are considerably heavier than the Georgian examples. It should also be remembered that many modern copies have been made of the Sunderland type wares, in particular the large bowls and jugs.

Sussex rustic ware

Regional or country pottery has been manufactured for centuries, although apart from pieces documenting specific occasions few have survived that can be easily attributed to a place of manufacture.

The literature on this subject is not considerable and I was particularly pleased to find a group of nineteenth-century papers published under the title *Sussex Industries* that included an interesting essay on pottery in the county. The anonymous and undated paper was reprinted from the *Sussex Advertiser* and is worthy of a wider audience:

'The name is a good one, for it describes the article faithfully. The ware is "rustic", suggestive of green woods and smiling hop-gardens, rustic in colour, rustic in style, rustic in the object which it represents. Its rusticity is however, attractive – by the combination of colours, by the somewhat roughly artistic moulding, and by its peculiarity of style. Where it is known it is liked. Specimens have been carried long distances to reap their meed of favour, and some pieces have, by Royal command, found their way into Her Majesty's household and Her Majesty's own use. The home of this peculiar product is the ancient cinqueport of Rye, a historic town picturesquely situated on the edge of the flat marshes which once were sea, into which it projects like a promontory of the higher, undulating, and remarkably pretty country which stretches northward into Kent, and westward into the finest part of Sussex. Deserted by the sea, although still in possession of communication with it by the conflux of three rivers, and thus enabled to carry on as of yore – though in attenuated dimensions – its native industry of shipbuilding, Rye, with its interesting and spacious old parish church, its land gate, and its Ypres tower, looks a relic of former ages, a small, self-contained community of last-century type. It is not cut off from contact with the outer world, for the railway carries visitors in on every market day – its markets being noted both for cattle and sheep – and the hopping season enlivens it with the influx of that wild and merry host who help to make out native beverage by reaping, in their own gipsy-like fashion, its most valued – and most frequently adulterated – ingredient. But on days when there is no market, and in seasons when there is no hopping, Rye is quiet enough.

'In its more primitive and more common form, pottery probably has been made at Rye as long as anywhere else. The inventor of the "rustic ware", the late Mr. F. Mitchell, made pots in the ordinary way at his father's works, still existing, until it occurred to him, some fourteen years ago, to strike out a new and original line of his own. He accordingly separated from his father, and set up independently, building up his own kiln, designed by himself. The manufacture of the ware is simple enough, and employs but few hands. The clay is mixed, well beaten, sifted with great care, once, twice, three times, and washed in the clay pan. This is filled every spring. When washed the clay looks like cream. It lies in the pan for months, dries, and then is stored for use–sufficient to last a year. When used it is weighed, so much to each article, and "spun" in the old-fashioned way upon the wheel. The "spinning", of course, gives scope for good workmanship, and such Mrs. Mitchell (whose husband died in 1875) has at her command. Many of the patterns are quaint, but they are all moulded with care and evident skill. The moulded pieces are left to dry until they can bear the weight of ornaments. These are then added, the ware is bis-cuited, glazed, kiln-dried–in saggers–and turned out for sale.

'This is all simple work. The peculiarity lies in the shape, in the combination of colours, and in the peculiar brown which forms the groundwork of the whole. The production of this brown is a trade-secret. It is inherent in the clay, not added by the glaze. It is produced by mixing very thoroughly the native material with Dorsetshire clay. The speckled and streaked appearance of the ware is attributable to the presence of two different materials which cannot wholly blend. It is a pleasant, "taking" sort of colour, setting off the green of the ornaments, the yellow occasionally introduced, to great advantage. But to the outsider, unacquainted with the details of the craft, the distinctive brown will appear less noteworthy than the shape and ornamentation of the articles, which are both exceedingly pleasing, and which represent the successful fruits of persevering study, an artistic mind, and a happy lightness of hand. Less pleasingly moulded, the ware, instead of securing for itself an honoured name in the trade, would presumably have proved a failure. We should here state that every piece turned out is moulded by hand. The wheel, on which the clay is "spun", is the only piece of machinery employed in the manufacture. The knife is used, principally for stippling, a wire for cutting, and moulds are resorted to for producing the ornaments in detail, flowers and leaves, hops and acorns; but all these ornaments, the basketwork–

where used–handles, &c., are put on by hand with very creditable taste and imitation of nature. A writer in the *Art Journal* some years ago bore complimentary witness to this praiseworthy proficiency, stating that "it is obvious that they (*scilicet* the moulder's fingers) have been directed by an artistic spirit." This commendation is deserved. The moulds for ornaments, we may add, are all taken from natural models–leaves from natural leaves, flowers from natural flowers, and so on. Both in respect of ornament, and of the shape of vessels, the late Mr. Mitchell and his surviving widow–who now conducts the works–have studied variety with capital results, but of course some patterns come out with more effect than others. One favourite pattern is the old Sussex "pig", familiar to Sussex potters from time immemorial. The inventive wag who was good-natured enough to assign to the county of Sussex as coat of arms "a pig, *proper*" (the emblem, we suppose, of Plenty coupled with Content), with the expressive motto appended, "Won't be druv", probably had this household ornament in his mind when he dispensed his heraldic honours in this irregular way. The useful office for which the pig was originally designed by our forefathers, and which it still faithfully discharges where ancient custom survives, is to receive the national beverage into its inside. It was usual for it to figure as a bridal present at wedding breakfasts. The head, which is somewhat insecurely fastened by means of a tapering peg inserted in two corresponding holes, made respectively in the head and the neck, takes off, and as the snout is perfectly flat, and capable of serving as a rest for the inverted headpiece, it is qualified to do service as a mug; the idea being that the new couple and their guests should drink "a hogshead of beer". Meanwhile the body serves as a jug or larger receptacle, discharging the liquor out of the neck. The tail is so conveniently curled upward as to assist rather than impede the laridiferous animal in resting–we cannot call it "sitting"–on his haunches, and thus one piece of pottery effectually performs, in its dismembered state, the useful services of two.

'Not a few patterns in use at Rye are faithful imitations of the Mycenae pottery brought to England by Dr. Schliemann, and not long ago exhibited at South Kensington. At the first suggestion it might appear questionable if this is altogether a happy choice, the new patch being made to fit on an old garment. But the result is far from unsatisfactory, indeed some pieces are unusually fine, and have accordingly been much admired, and we are disposed to agree with Mrs. Mitchell, that it is a sound principle to perpetuate the antique forms, and bring home to our living generation the fact that the classic patterns admired in museums were at one time really in every-day use, and intended for every-day purposes. Mrs. Mitchell at present makes "Trojan" pottery in no fewer than eighteen different shapes, every one of them copied from the Mycenae collection. Some, for instance the triangular jugs, present to modern eyes a quaint appearance; most come out remarkably well when moulded in Sussex clay. Other models Mrs. Mitchell has borrowed, with, perhaps, even more satisfactory results, from later times and nearer neighbours. Thus one favourite pattern is in imitation of the French Valérie ware. Another favourite article is the Belgian candlestick, first suggested for imitation by the Rev. J. S. Northcote, the son of the Right Hon. Member for North Devon. A pattern to be met with wherever the ware is seen, is a peculiar kind of bag, evidently moulded on a real bag. This strikes many observers as an odd, if original, shape. The fact is, that it is an imitation of a Russian pattern, brought home by the Duke of Edinburgh, and recommended to Mrs. Mitchell as a model by Mr. J. S. Hardy, the late Member for Rye. There are other candlesticks besides the Belgian pattern, some rather elaborate, many certainly in good taste, and all in frequent practical use. Another species of ware selling well are the Japanese jugs, which are made in different sizes, and prove no less useful than ornamental. One very peculiar shape has been christened "Sussex pails". These are pails resting on a flat bottom or tray, with a hoop handle from the bottom to above the top. Then there are antique lamps, carpenter's bags–most useful as receptacles for flowers–flower-baskets, pilgrim's bottles, Cambridge jugs, and many more. One very peculiar shape goes by the name of "rustic stumps", representing the stump of a tree, stippled with a knife to produce roughness, and used for holding flowers, or else as a jug. Another speciality, original if quaint, is the twisted ware–"folding jugs", as Mrs. Mitchell calls them–having a spiral turn, produced by twisting the jug while soft, and drying it in this condition. A resemblance with the famed Palissy ware has suggested an imitation of Palissy's "reptile" plates. These take a deal of trouble, but they are really works of art.

'As regards pattern, we are, however, inclined to award the palm to those objects which, in shape as well as in make, bear a strong local stamp upon them. Mrs. Mitchell moulds her clay very successfully in imitation of all sorts of leaves and flowers, fuchsias, passion flowers, and what not, but the most telling effect is produced by the rich clusters of flowering hops or the homely sprigs of oak bearing their proper crop of acorns. These are mostly disposed upon appropriate objects, and it is by virtue of these chiefly, we think, that the reputation of the Sussex pottery may be expected to spread. We ought also to mention some really artistic representations of green wheat-ears, which are very effective on a brown ground. They help to preserve the "rustic" character of the ware. We have been shown in Mrs. Mitchell's private collection far more elaborate objects, flower-stands, wreaths, and very charming – but laborious – basketwork (which we should like to see, on account of its fine effect, more frequently made) – but it is the jugs and mugs encircled with clusters of hops, and strongly suggestive of the beverage made of that peculiarly indigenous plant, and for which they are intended – the George II jug, in its simple but attractive form, set off by a thick wreath of hops – the very tasteful baskets decorated with the same native green – moreover such objects as cheese-dishes, and simple trays or plates bordered or ornamented with sprigs of green – it is these comparatively homely but particularly appropriate and "local"-looking objects, which seem to us most deserving of notice, and most calculated to extend the use of the "ware". It must be borne in mind that however "taking" is the pottery, it is not pottery of artistically the very highest rank, and its models and uses should be selected and assigned accordingly. There is not the same exquisite finish, the plastic imitativeness, the artistic execution about it which distinguishes the best earthenware, say Doulton or Wedgwood. But it has a catching "local" look, which grows upon one, and is quite artistic enough to qualify for a prominent place among our native manufacturers. The more it is known the more popular, we are sure, will it become. Greater popularity is not now sought after, because the ware is sold as fast as ever it is made, and the demand is apt, if anything, to outstrip the circumscribed productive power of the existing establishment. But there is no reason why the latter should not be expanded and rendered capable of turning out much larger quantities of ware. It might benefit the neighbourhood in which it is made, if this were done, and it would help to secure to the County of Sussex an honourable place among the industrial counties of England.'

79 *Above:* Wedgwood Queensware group with transfer decoration by Sadler and Green of Liverpool, *c.* 1770. The print on the teapot depicts the death of General Wolfe.

80 *Below:* Part of the famous Wedgwood service made for the Empress Catherine II of Russia, *c.* 1774.

84

85

Chapter 5

Josiah Wedgwood

81 *Above:* Wedgwood jasper pieces that demonstrate the rich colour range of this fine stoneware. Eighteenth century. Jasper was produced in six basic colours: black, green, blue, dark blue, lilac and yellow. Other colours were also experimented with.

In the last chapter I mentioned the Potteries with their peasant craftsmen, unorganised labour, non-existent sales force and inadequate communications. It was into this setting that Josiah Wedgwood emerged as a giant among European potters. His is now a household name throughout the world, and his ideas regarding production, the management of men and of factories, and division of labour have had a major bearing on mass production today.

The ceramicist William Burton said this of Wedgwood: '. . . his influence was so powerful, and his personality dominant, that all other English potters worked on the principles that he had laid down, and thus a fresh influence and a new direction was given to the pottery of England and of the civilised world. He is the only potter of whom it may be truly said that the whole subsequent course of pottery manufacture has been influenced by his individuality, skill and taste.'

The foundation stone of the Wedgwood Memorial Institute in Burslem was laid in 1863 by William Gladstone, who was then Chancellor of the Exchequer. Mr Gladstone said of Wedgwood in his address:

'. . . he was the greatest man who ever, in any age or in any country, applied himself to the important work in uniting art and industry.'

82 *Below:* The Wedgwood family in the grounds of Etruria Hall. This portrait painted in oils on a panel by George Stubbs in 1780 depicts the master potter, Josiah Wedgwood, FRS, and his wife Sarah, with seven of their eight children. Josiah and Sarah sit under a tree. The children on horseback are, from left: Thomas (a pioneer of photography); Susannah (who became the mother of Charles Darwin, biologist and author of *The Origin of Species*); Josiah (the second son who inherited the pottery company); and John (the eldest son and a founder of the Royal Horticultural Society). Josiah Wedgwood and Sons Ltd., Barlaston, Stoke-on-Trent.

During the span of Josiah Wedgwood's life (1730-1795) he brought about a revolution that went even beyond the bounds of pottery. To look at a map of Staffordshire in the early eighteenth century and to note the names of the individual potters with their crude pot-banks scattered across the countryside is like reading the index to a whole volume devoted to ceramic history. The Wedgwood family were already among their number, for several generations of Wedgwoods had earned their living as potters, selling their wares, as did their neighbours, to the casual tinkers who were the principal buyers.

It was at the Churchyard Pottery, Burslem, that Josiah Wedgwood was born in 1730, the youngest of the twelve children of Thomas and Mary Wedgwood. The exact date of his birth is not known, but it would have been very close to the day of his baptism, 12 July, as at that period little time was allowed to elapse between birth and baptism, because of the high infant mortality.

A brief sketch of Wedgwood's career is useful to show the scale of his achievement and also the manner in which his work with ceramics evolved. At the age of six he began a daily walk of three miles to school at Newcastle-under-Lyme, and it was there that the family also attended the Unitarian Meeting House which was always to be an important part of Josiah Wedgwood's life.

Life was certainly not easy for Josiah, but although he had to leave school at the age of nine when his father died, he was able to read, do simple arithmetic and write well. Then, after working at the family pot-bank for five years, he became afflicted, like so many others in eighteenth-century England, with smallpox. It left him with a weakened right knee that was to trouble him for many years and it also meant that it was no longer possible for him to operate a potter's wheel. Perhaps the most bitter blow of all was that his eldest brother refused to take him into partnership. This time of Wedgwood's life must have appeared to him like the end, in fact it was barely the beginning.

For two years he worked with John Harrison at the Cliff-bank Pottery and then, like many another fortunate potter, he met Thomas Whieldon, the most prominent potter of the day. Wedgwood and Whieldon entered into a partnership that lasted five years, years in which Wedgwood discovered all he could of the contemporary wares, the white stonewares, the agates and the tortoiseshells, that largely dominated the output of the partnership. Attractive as these items were, and still are, Wedgwood felt the necessity of improving the body of the clays being used, and of bringing about improvements in glaze, colour and design—what he called 'elegance of form'. As he surveyed the products of the potteries he wrote, 'I saw the field was spacious, and the soil so good as to promise an ample recompense to anyone who should labour diligently'. The words have something of a Churchillian ring and, appropriately, he followed them with action.

In 1759 Wedgwood started his own business at the Ivy House Works at Burslem, renting the premises for £10 a year from his cousins who lived nearby. He invented a new green

83 Queensware teacaddy, with transfer printed decoration. Wedgwood, *c.* 1770. Victoria and Albert Museum, London.

wedgwood

Probably the first mark, and supposedly used at Burslem, 1759-69

WEDCWOOD

Very rare mark, used at the Bell Works, 1764-69

WEDGWOOD

Wedgwood

Mark used in various sizes, 1759-69

84 Queensware teapot with flowers and leaves hand painted in enamels. Wedgwood, *c.* 1770. Merseyside County Museums, Liverpool.

Earliest form of the Wedgwood and Bentley stamp, 1769

Circular stamp, placed around screw of certain bases, but never on jasper ware, 1769-80

Wedgwood
& Bentley
356

Mark used on Wedgwood and Bentley intaglios, 1769-80

glaze which was ideally suited to the cauliflower-shaped teapots and the Rococo style wares of the day. Wedgwood's pottery grew and flourished. In 1762 he moved to the Brick House pot-bank later known as the Bell Works, for the workmen instead of being summoned by the blowing of a horn were called to work by a bell. His experiments with clays led to great improvements on those used by earlier potters such as John Astbury, and the development of a strong, light, elegant creamware began to claim most of his time. It bore fruit in the now celebrated Queensware, so called in honour of Queen Charlotte and her patronage. Creamware was to lay the basis of his fortune and create the finance necessary to carry out his later projects and experiments. It was so successful that within three years Wedgwood was using an agent in London. His creamwares were left plain or either painted by hand or transfer printed by Sadler and Green in Liverpool. With such simple, clean lines these strong and useful wares are as much at home in the twentieth century as they were two hundred years ago.

The Brick House factory not only saw the rise of creamware but also the flourishing of a vital friendship. During one of his visits to Liverpool in 1762, Wedgwood injured his already infirm knee. The pain was crippling, and, unable to ride, he was forced to take to his bed. His doctor, Matthew Turner, then introduced Wedgwood to a man named Thomas Bentley. Although of similar ages Bentley was in every way different to Wedgwood: he was a Liverpool merchant of sophisticated tastes, with a wide knowledge and a strong interest in

85 Portrait in oils of Thomas Bentley, attributed to the artist Joseph Wright of Derby, and painted in 1775. Bentley was Wedgwood's Partner from 1769 to 1780. His taste, social contacts and knowledge of the arts did much to ensure the success of the firm.

European and classical art. Undoubtedly it was Bentley who opened the eyes of Wedgwood to the classical collections of Sir William Hamilton, British Consul to the Kingdom of Naples. It would have been Bentley who became aware of the beginnings of the neo-classical movement. In 1766 Wedgwood proposed a partnership, and such was their friendship it was many years before they thought it necessary to sign a formal partnership agreement. It was Bentley who took charge of the London warehouse and showrooms, Wedgwood being among the first to have showrooms in the capital.

The relationship between Wedgwood and Bentley was far more than a mere business association and when apart they corresponded almost daily. Wedgwood once wrote of Bentley's letters that 'the very feel of them even before the seal is broke, cheers my heart and does me good. They inspire me with taste, emulation and everything that is necessary for the production of fine things.' Sadly, few of Bentley's letters to Wedgwood have survived but the Wedgwood correspondence is invaluable to all who are interested in Wedgwood and the potteries. The letters are also interspersed with lines that testify to the good fellowship between them. Once when Bentley moved house Wedgwood wrote to him: 'Do not be in haste to set your second garden. I will come and help you dig and weed, and sow and gather, and we will be joint gardeners as well as joint potters.'

In the spring of 1768 Wedgwood's knee again became inflamed and this time there was no doubt what had to be done. The amputation was successfully carried out (without benefit of anaesthetics) and Wedgwood made a good recovery and in due course an artificial wooden leg was fitted. With his better health, new vistas opened for Wedgwood and Bentley. Thanks to the dowry of his wife Sara, Wedgwood purchased for £3,000 an estate between Hanley and Newcastle-under-Lyme. He built a house for himself and a short distance away he constructed the largest pottery manufactory in the world, which as a factory was second in size only to the Soho works of Matthew Boultin in Birmingham. Wedgwood called the factory Etruria, in honour of that part of Italy where so much ancient pottery was then being unearthed.

The factory opened on 13 June 1769 and to mark the event Wedgwood made six vases with Thomas Bentley turning the potter's wheel and Wedgwood throwing and turning the pots. These vases are known as the 'First day vases' and bear a Latin inscription meaning 'The Arts of Etruria are reborn'. The

86 Queensware jelly mould complete with decorated centre-piece. The painted flowers would be visible through the clear translucent jelly. Eighteenth century.

Etruria of ancient Italy knew nothing like this, with spacious modelling and throwing rooms making it possible to retain quality while large quantities were being produced. The completion of a combined dinner and tea service in creamware for the Empress Catherine II of Russia was a massive advertisement as well as a great achievement for Wedgwood. The service consisted of 952 pieces decorated with 1,244 original paintings of English landscapes; the manufacturing costs were very nearly £3,000. Before the service left for Russia it was exhibited in Wedgwood's London showroom in Greek Street where it proved a great attraction.

For most people the epitome of Wedgwood is jasper ware, which first appeared in 1774. An unglazed vitreous (highly fired, close bodied) stoneware, it was manufactured in various shades of blue, yellow, green, lilac, maroon, black or white. It only emerged after some 10,000 attempts and most of the trial pieces together with Wedgwood's personal notes are still in the Wedgwood archive – no wonder he wrote desperately in his experiment book when success seemed far away 'I am going mad'.

Wedgwood's search for perfection was unceasing. He invented the pyrometer and so became the first man to devise an instrument that would accurately record the high temperature of a kiln. The man with only three years' formal education was made a Fellow of the Royal Society. He experimented with clays from as far afield as China and North America and gradually the ill-organised Staffordshire potteries were set new standards and transformed into a major industry. George Stubbs painted the Wedgwood family at Etruria Hall and Sir Joshua Reynolds, first President of the Royal Academy, painted his portrait.

Wedgwood's strong Unitarian beliefs led him to oppose the slave trade, as a letter to Benjamin Franklin dated 29 February 1788 clearly shows:

'I embrace the opportunity of a packet making up by my friend Phillip to inclose for the use of yourself and friends a few Cameos on a subject which I am happy to acquaint you is daily more and more taking possession of mens minds on this side of the Atlantic as well as with you.

'It gives me great pleasure to be embarked on this occasion in the same great and good cause with you, and I ardently hope for the final completion of our wishes. This will be an epoch before unknown to the World, and while relief is given to millions of our fellow Creatures immediately the object of it, the subject of freedom will be more canvassed and better understood in the enlightened nations.'

87 The fine black basalt ware shown above and in the opposite column was an achievement of which Josiah Wedgwood was particularly proud, saying that it was 'sterling, and will last forever'.

The packet of cameos referred to in the letter was a number of the medallions modelled by Hackwood and designed by Josiah Wedgwood that show a manacled negro slave kneeling with his hands raised while around the edge of the medallion is the inscription 'Am I not a man and a brother?'

Wedgwood had thousands of these cameos or slave medallions as they are called made and distributed them free to anyone who was concerned with the anti-slavery movement. He also supported the Americans during the War of Independence and in a letter to Erasmus Darwin he wrote:

'I know you will rejoice with me in the glorious revolution which has taken place in France. The Politicians tell me that as a manufacturer I shall be ruined if France has her liberty, but I am willing to take my chance in that respect, nor yet do I see that the happiness of one Nation includes in it the misery of its next neighbour.'

At Etruria Wedgwood built houses for his work-force and was the prime mover behind the development of the Trent and Mersey Canal which linked Etruria with the port of Liverpool, a move which cut the factory's road transport costs from $10\frac{1}{2}$d ($4\frac{1}{2}$p) per ton mile to $1\frac{1}{2}$d ($\frac{1}{2}$p) per ton mile by canal.

Deeply involved in the scientific developments of his age, Josiah Wedgwood supplied Joseph Priestley with ceramic tubes and retorts for his scientific experiments, and he installed a James Watt steam engine to drive a special lathe. When he died in 1795 he left not only a personal fortune of over half a million pounds and a large factory, but also a whole tradition both in English pottery and in industrial organisation. He also created a dynasty. His son John was a founder of the Royal Horticultural Society, Josiah junior inherited the pottery, Thomas was a pioneer of photography and his daughter Susannah became the mother of Charles Darwin, the biologist, evolutionist and author of *The Origin of Species*.

Black basalt

The early and crude black pottery named 'Egyptian black' was one of the first wares to which Wedgwood had turned his attention. In 1768 he developed the fine-grained, unglazed, hard black stoneware that is called black basalt. The rich hue of the basalt was created by staining the body with manganese dioxide and cobalt. The basalt wares could be decorated further by being polished on a jeweller's wheel after firing or by the addition of red and white encaustic enamel colours in Greek and Roman styles before a second firing. This basalt is capable of resisting acids and was frequently used as a touch-stone to test the quality of silver and gold. At this period gentlemen were buying books and developing their private libraries, and black basalt life-sized busts of classical and modern authors were popular as decoration as well as cheaper than bronze or marble originals. Some vases were bronzed but these are rare. Fluting and lathe-turning was an easy form of decoration to apply; moulded decorations in low relief took longer as they had first to be moulded and then undercut to make the details precise.

At the same time there arose the taste for collecting ancient and Renaissance camoes, cut from semi-precious stones. Obviously this taste could only be cultivated by the wealthy and many copies were produced in glass, white plaster and red sulphur. Again Wedgwood used contemporary taste to his advantage by reproducing the ancient intaglio designs. Here is an entry from the Wedgwood and Bentley catalogue of 1779: 'The Intaglios in artificial basalts are most excellent seals; being exact impressions from the finest gems; and therefore much truer than any engraved copies can be, with the singular advantage of being little inferior in hardness to the gems themselves.

'In this composition Cameos may be converted into seals without losing the Drawing, the Spirit and Delicacy of the original work; so that gentlemen may have a great variety of seals at small expense, or have an opportunity of making collections of perfect and durable copies of the choicest Gems.'

Between 1800 and 1810, decoration in the Chinese *famille rose* style was applied to black basalt ware and is known as the 'chrysanthemum pattern'. Of black basalt Wedgwood wrote: 'The black is stirling and will last forever'.

Rosso Antico

This red stoneware dates from the early 1760s and is reminiscent of the early Staffordshire red wares. This stoneware was also decorated in much the same way as black basalt.

Variegated wares

These fall into two groups. The earliest was made of cream-coloured earthenware with a marbled surface. The tortoiseshell effect was obtained by dusting metallic oxide on to the surface of the body, and could also be achieved by combing or sponging on splashes of colour. The later type consists of various coloured clays that were kneaded together with the intention of imitating stones such as agate, onyx or marble.

Cane ware

Useful and ornamental wares were made from cane colour earthenware, and frequently a bamboo effect was simulated. Another form of cane ware became known as 'ceramic pastry' because of its use in replacing edible pie-crust. During the Napoleonic wars flour became scarce and costly and one of the immediate results of this was that the game pie served at table in its thick and ornamental cut pie-crust dish became very expensive. Wedgwood's pie dish of 'ceramic pastry' was not only more attractive than most artistic attempts in real pastry, but was also represented as a great saving in time, it was in fact what might be termed the first oven-to-table ware.

Jasper ware

The production of jasper, which is technically a stone ware, was finally perfected in 1774 following years of experiment in the search for the right ingredients. It is a dense white highly vitrified ware that possesses some characteristics of porcelain; that is, when thinly potted it is sometimes translucent. One of the essential ingredients of jasper is barium sulphate. Always unglazed, jasper could be stained lilac, yellow, maroon, green, blue or black to provide the ideal background for applied moulded classical reliefs or portraits. For Josiah Wedgwood it represents his highest achievement as far as colour is concerned, and his uses of it are many and varied.

Portrait medallions, classical panels, jewellery, sword hilts, as well as all manner of vases, were made in jasper. The artists who produced the designs were all highly skilled, among them John Flaxman, William Hackwood, Lady Templeton and George Stubbs. The architect Robert Adam was quick to seize upon Wedgwood's ceramic interpretations of the neo-classic and he frequently used Wedgwood jaspers as features in his designs, especially in fireplaces.

The most celebrated example of jasper is probably Wedgwood's replica of the Portland Vase. This was originally known as the Barberini Vase, and was found enclosed in a sarcophagus of fine workmanship in a burial chamber beneath a mound of earth, 3 miles (4·8 km) from Rome. The sarcophagus was placed in the museum at Rome and the $10\frac{1}{4}$ inch (260 mm) high vase

found its way to the library of the Barberini family in the eighteenth century and was later purchased at considerable expense in Italy by the great connoisseur and collector Sir William Hamilton, who brought it to England in the December of 1784. The fame of the vase had long preceded its arrival and the Dowager Duchess of Portland, a collector on a massive scale, was the first person to visit him at his London hotel. Within a few days she began negotiations for the purchase of the vase through Sir William's niece, who was a Maid of Honour to the Queen. The arrangements were conducted in great secrecy as Mrs Delany, who acted for the Duchess, recorded: '. . . by whispers, signs, confabulations in their parlours and bed chambers, and by notes'. It was Horace Walpole who described the Duchess as: 'A sober Lady but much intoxicated by empty vases'.

Following direct talks between Sir William and the Duchess, the sale of the Barberini Vase was eventually settled. From then until her death the following year, on 17 July 1785, the vase was not seen by anyone apart from a few tried and trusted friends. The Portland family had previously voiced their disapproval of the large sums of money she willingly spent on her personal museum, and it was for this reason that she tried so carefully to keep her latest purchase a secret. When the Duke disposed of the museum he wished to retain at least some of its treasures and although Wedgwood had already tried to buy the vase, the museum was sold at the Duchess's residence in Whitehall. The sale lasted thirty-five days beginning on 24 April and ending on 7 June, 1786. There were 4,155 lots and the vase was the last lot in the sale. It is believed that Wedgwood and the Duke of Portland had come to a previous understanding that the Duke should buy the vase and that Wedgwood should have it on loan to make a copy. The representative of the Duke of Portland bought in the vase for the sum of £1,029, and three days after its sale, it passed into Wedgwood's care upon his receipt of possession and promise of return:

'I do hereby acknowledge to have borrowed and received from His Grace the Duke of Portland, the vase described in the 4155 lot of the catalogue of the Portland Museum, and also the cameo medallion of the head of Augustus Caesar being the lot of the same catalogue and both sold by Messrs. Skinner on the 7th day of the present month of June, 1786 & I do hereby promise to deliver back the said Vase and Cameo in safety into the hands of His Grace upon demand.

Witness my hand this 10th day of June, 1786.

Jos Wedgwood.

(Signed in the presence of)

Thos Byerley.'

The Portland Vase is without doubt one of the great works of art in the world. Once it was in the hands of Wedgwood, and closer examination had enabled him to understand its intricate beauty, his normal self-assurance began to be undermined by doubt. He wrote a letter to Sir William Hamilton setting out the difficulties of the task and sought his advice on a number of points. It seems likely that Sir William advised the pursuit of a copy as close to the original as possible, although correcting the work of damage or decay. Wedgwood's attitude is reflected in this extract from one of his letters:

'. . . now that I can indulge myself with full and repeated examinations of the original work itself, my crest is much fallen and I should scarcely muster sufficient resolution to proceed if I had not too precipitately perhaps pledged myself to many of my friends to attempt it in the best manner I am able. Being so pledged, I must proceed . . .'

Wedgwood then continues:

'Several gentlemen have urged me to make my copies of the vase by subscription, & have honoured me with their names for that purpose; but I tell them with great truth, that I am extremely diffident of my ability to perform the task they kindly impose upon me; and they shall be perfectly at liberty when they see the copies, to take or refuse them; and on these terms I accept subscriptions, chiefly to regulate the time of delivering out the copies, in rotation, according to the dates on which they honour me with their names.'

Wedgwood's tenacity was to prove equal to the task. He discovered that the original was made of glass rather than hardstone, as had been assumed. The glass itself was of a dark blue, so much so that unless held to a strong light it appeared to be black, while the figures in white bas-relief are also of glass. Even today much inconclusive discussion continues regarding the interpretation of the legends depicted by the figures. The modelling for the copy was carried out by Henry Webber, but it was the task of giving the exact body colouring to the jasper that presented the real problem. After four years of experiment Wedgwood achieved his first copies. Sir Joshua Reynolds, after carefully examining one of them, described it as 'a correct and faithful imitation both in the general effect and the most minute details of the part'. The very first vase was submitted to Wedgwood's great friend, Dr Darwin, for his inspection. He was instructed to show it to no one but his family, but as he later wrote to Wedgwood: 'I have disobeyed you . . . how can I possess a jewel, and not communicate the pleasure to a few Derby philosophers?'

In 1810 the Portland Vase was deposited by the third Duke of Portland in the British Museum on permanent loan and it has remained there ever since, although the Museum purchased the vase from the Portland family in 1945. It is the finest known example of 'cameo glass' and dates from early in the first century AD, and because the figures in white relief depict the marriage of Peleus and Thetis, it was probably originally intended as a wedding gift.

On 7 February 1845 a tragedy of major proportions struck the Antiquities Department of the British Museum. A certain William Lloyd, having picked up a Babylonian stone sculpture, deliberately smashed the glass case containing the Portland Vase, shattering it into over two hundred pieces. The act of this madman appeared to have destroyed the great work of art for ever, but with the help of Josiah Wedgwood's copy the Museum, with infinite patience, was able to repair the vase, and in March 1846 it was again on exhibition. As so often happens good followed disaster, and the smashing of the vase drew massive public attention to it. It was for this reason that after 1845 Wedgwood began to make further copies in various sizes. Unlike the original issue, these later copies have the Wedgwood mark and do not include the medallion of the female head on the base which is such a superb feature of the original vase and of the original series of copies. Today the Portland Vase is used as a symbol of Wedgwood and is incorporated in the company's back stamp on fine bone china. The Wedgwood copies still fetch within the region of £20,000 when they appear at auction.

Creamware

The finest creamware of Josiah Wedgwood was superior to anything of its kind already in existence, and firmly established his business. His products were light and white, and could compete with the wares of porcelain manufacturers.

89 Creamware transfer-printed plate by Sadler and Green of Liverpool.

Thus a demand was created for such wares, and other manufacturers became very interested, particularly in Leeds and Liverpool, where they were worked on by the great firm of transfer printers, Sadler and Green, who formed a partnership in 1761 to deal with the mass printing of creamwares that followed the opening of an account with Josiah Wedgwood.

Much creamware, however, was left plain white. Such pieces sold because of good design alone, but white was also an ideal ground on which to have painted personal requests. This was particularly the case with marriage jugs or tankards and christening mugs, but it also applied to jugs commemorating any number of events of family, work, society, or volunteer force. Other jugs were printed or painted with various verses. A great deal of military history is also recorded on creamware, for example the death of General Wolfe at Quebec in 1759, and the victories of Wellington and Nelson. This tradition was carried on through the nineteenth century on jugs and mugs of all kinds of ceramic body; Samuel Alcock & Co. of Hill Pottery, Burslem, produced a fine Crimea jug in 1855. All commemorative creamware is very popular with collectors.

Once Wedgwood's success was seen a host of other manufacturers also launched into creamware production: John Turner, Josiah Spode, William Adams and Sunderland among them. Liverpool potters made good creamware but that of Leeds was at least the equal of Wedgwood. The Leeds pieces were as light and occasionally lighter than Wedgwood, although there is a tendency for the Leeds glaze to appear green where it has run and gathered in crevices.

90 *Far left:* Creamware coffee pot with enamelled decoration. Leeds, *c.* 1765.

91 *Above:* Creamware teapot, Leeds, *c.* 1767.

92 Creamware sparrow-beak milk jug and cover with a crossover handle so typical of both Wedgwood and Leeds. Leeds, *c.* 1780.

93 Creamware centre-piece with detachable nut baskets. Wedgwood.

Tea and coffee ware was made together with baskets and bowls. Some of the larger pieces were decorated by pierced work. Pierced borders were also in favour, although at Leeds dishes and plate rims are often found with feather-moulded edges touched with blue. Cross-over handles are also used.

Messrs. Hartley, Greens & Co., the Leeds potters, issued pattern books from time to time during the late eighteenth and early nineteenth centuries. These books show a surprising range of wares, from spoons to chamber pots, table centres, ink stands and decorative vases. That they were ready to fulfil private orders in respect of decoration is made clear by the wording on the cover of their pattern book:

DESIGNS

of

SUNDRY ARTICLES

of

QUEEN'S OR CREAM-COLOUR'D EARTHEN-WARE

MANUFACTURED BY

HARTLEY, GREENS, AND CO.

at

LEEDS POTTERY

with

A GREAT VARIETY OF OTHER ARTICLES

THE SAME ENAMEL'D, PRINTED OR ORNAMENTED WITH

GOLD TO ANY PATTERN; ALSO WITH COATS OF ARMS,

CYPHERS, LANDSCAPES, &C. &C.

There is no better way of appreciating the rich variety of creamware itself than by quoting some of the verses so often found on it.

On a puzzle jug:

> *Within this jug there is good liquor*
> *T'is fit for Parson or for Vicar;*
> *But how to drink and not to spill,*
> *Will try the utmost of your skill.*

On a jug dated 1835 and decorated with agricultural implements:

> *Let the wealthy and the great*
> *Roll in splendour and state*
> *I envy them not I declare it*
> *I eat my own lamb*
> *My own chicken and ham*
> *I shear my own fleece and I wear it*

101

> *I have lawns I have bowers*
> *I have fruits I have flowers*
> *The lark is my morning alarmer*
> *So you jolly boys now*
> *Here's God speed the plough*
> *Long life and success to the farmer.*

94 *Above:* Two fine creamware jugs, made in Liverpool and with a typical Liverpool shape, *c.* 1786.

95 *Below:* Part of a bone china tea service with japan decoration. Wedgwood, early nineteenth century.

On a drinking mug:

> *Come my old friend and take a Pot*
> *But mark now what I say*
> *While that thou drinkest thy neighbours health*
> *Drink not thine own away*
> *It but too often is the case*
> *While we sit o'er a Pot*
> *We kindly wish our friend good Health*
> *Our own is quite forgot.*

On a marriage jug:

> *In courtship Strephon careful*
> *hands his lass*
> *Over a stile a child with ease*
> *might pass*
> *But wedded Strephon now neglects*
> *his dame*
> *Tumble or not to him tis all the same.*

On a lustre wall plaque:

> *May Peace and Plenty*
> *On our Nation Smile*
> *And Trade with Commerce*
> *Bless the British Isle.*

On a Staffordshire frog mug:

> *Tho' malt and venom*
> *Seem united*
> *Don't break my pot*
> *Nor be affrighted.*

On a tankard:

> *Here's to the maid of bashful fifteen*
> *Likewise to the matron of fifty*
> *Here's to the bold and extravagant Queen*
> *And here's to the housewife that's thrifty.*

On another tankard:

> *In Country Village lives a Vicar*
> *Fond as all are of Tithes and Liquor.*

On a jug of 1793:

The Martyr of Equality
'Behold the progress of the French System'

Here I see the victim bleeding
By a brother doom'd to die
All in vain for pity pleading
Pity dare not lift her eye.

May Britain a true
Their rights pursue
And e'er espouse the cause
Of Church and King
And every Thing
That constitutes their Laws.

Portrait medallions

One of the most collectable areas of eighteenth-century Wedgwood production is in portrait medallions. These include the likenesses of classical figures and also of Wedgwood's contemporaries, and represent a whole gallery of portraits ranging from royalty and republicans, to actors, politicians, scientists and artists. Hundreds of such medallions were made and the tradition has continued until the present day. Wedgwood employed a number of modellers but was particularly pleased with the work of William Hackwood and in 1776 was wishing that 'we had half a dozen more Hackwoods'. Other modellers were John Flaxman, RA, whose services were secured by Bentley, Joachim Smith and John Charles Lochee, who also worked for other concerns. James Tassie was also a source for Wedgwood medallions; this brilliant gem engraver, together with Dr Henry Quin, invented a composition suitable for casting cameos, intaglios and portrait medallions. Although Wedgwood and Tassie were rivals in this field, they remained good friends. George Stubbs designed reliefs of horses, and the work of Lady Templeton and Lady Beauclark are distinctive when employed on sentimental classical reliefs, mainly of women and children.

96 *Opposite:* Wedgwood portrait medallions form a unique series of historical portraits, the first of them being offered for sale in 1773. This group includes Captain Cook and William Pitt. The larger portrait medallion is of Erasmus Darwin (1731-1802), the botanist and physician and a lifelong friend of Josiah Wedgwood.

Wedgwood did not enter the arena of porcelain production, but some excellent bone china was produced by his son Josiah junior between 1812 and 1822; many of the teapots and jugs of tea services were frequently derived from silver shapes of the day. Josiah Wedgwood's grandson revived the production of bone china at the factory in 1878.

Unquestionably there were many important commercial factors that contributed to Josiah Wedgwood's success, and the lessons he learned and put into practice became examples not only for his contemporaries in the Potteries and those who followed them but in many other fields of industry as well.

Etruria was a symbol of change, and the small family potters could no longer cope with demand or the new sophisticated potting techniques. Wedgwood set about solving his problems with strict factory discipline and the division of labour: he kept individual workshops quite separate and believed that the production of what he termed useful works should be kept well apart from that of ornamental works. He trained the men

97 Transfer-printed plate inscribed 'Keep within compass and you shall be sure to avoid many troubles which others endure'. John Aynsley of Lane End, c. 1790. Victoria and Albert Museum, London.

106

to one task, raising the quality of work in the process, and men were paid strictly according to their expertise. The modeller, William Hackwood, might earn forty-two shillings (£2·10) per week, while other painters could earn as little as a shilling (5p). The work force of the potteries had previously enjoyed great freedom, being able to move from one task to another, but under Wedgwood this came to an end. He often needed trained painters and modellers, and he realised that it would be necessary to train workers rather than face the continual problem of trying to find skilled labour on a jobbing basis. He employed artists of renown to produce designs, but he made sure that their contact with his permanent work force was kept to a minimum, for he felt that they were a disrupting influence to his scheme of factory management. He wrote: 'Oh! for a dozen good and humble modellers at Etruria for a couple of months. What creations, renovations and generations should we make! well – fair and softley we must proceed with our own natural forces, for I will have no fine modellers here, though I seem to wish for them they would corrupt and ruin us all.' He took the local semi-skilled potters and made what he called 'mere men' into artists. Five years before his death, nearly a quarter of his work force were apprentices, and he also took on girls.

Wedgwood banned drinking and created a system of fines for transgressors. He insisted upon regular attendance at work, punctuality and the highest standards of cleanliness. He shook off the general belief that a pottery involved waste, dirty conditions and work by unscientific rule-of-thumb. He also invented the first clocking-in system:

'To save the trouble of the porters going round, tickets may perhaps be used, in the following manner – Let some sheets of pasteboard paper be printed with the names of all the work people, and the names cut off, about the size of half a card. Let each person take two of these tickets with him when he leaves work every evening; one of which he is to deliver into a box when he goes through the lodge in the morning, and the other when he returns from dinner. The porter then, instead of going round the works in the morning, looks over these tickets only; & if he finds any deficiency, goes to such places only where the deficiency appears. If the persons have neglected or refused to deliver their tickets on going through, they are to be admonished the first time, the second time to pay a small fine to the poor box. . . . It will be necessary to have divisions for the tickets in alphabetic order, for the greater facility of giving them out.'

It was indeed an industrial revolution. He introduced a clerk of weight and measures who would weigh the correct weight of clay for use for particular wares. When walking through the factory he is said to have smashed any pots that he regarded as being substandard, writing with chalk on the bench of the men responsible: 'This won't do for Josiah Wedgwood'. His attention to cleanliness had a motive not readily appreciated by many of the work force. When going through registers at St John's Church, Burslem, recently, I found the brief comment 'potters rot' against the names of some of the dead. 'Potters rot' was the name given to lead poisoning and it is why Wedgwood did not allow workmen to eat in the dipping room and insisted that 'a pail of water with soap and a towel and a brush for the nails to be always at hand'. The men and boys working in such areas wore smocks as a form of protective clothing, and Wedgwood insisted that floors and other surfaces should be washed or sponged and never brushed when dry, to avoid creating clouds of dust.

Having trained his work force, Wedgwood went to considerable lengths to keep them. It was not merely the competition for skilled men locally that he sought to avoid, but the hiring by agents on behalf of manufacturers in Europe and America. He warned his men that promises made in this country might not be kept when they went abroad and he also appealed to their sense of loyalty:

'You must by this time be fully convinced, how delusive the offers held out to you are, and how contrary it would be to your own interest to accept them. But supposing for a moment, that with regard to your own particular persons there was a real and lasting advantage. Would it have no weight with you to think, that you were ruining a trade, which had taken the united efforts of some thousands of people, for more than an age, to bring to the perfection it has now attained? a perfection no where else to be found – an object exciting at once the envy and emulation of all Europe! but they will both ever be harmless to us whilst we are true to ourselves: for Englishmen, in arts and manufacturers as well as in arms, can only be conquered by Englishmen: the enemy must first gain over some traitors and renegades from among ourselves, before they can attain any decisive advantage. Is there a man among you then who will stand forth, and acknowledge himself to be that traitor to his country and fellow workmen? who will openly avow, that for the sake of a paltry addition to his own wages for few years, he would betray their interests, and wantonly throw

98 Creamware portrait plate, Admiral Lord Nelson, Staffordshire, *c.* 1810. Victoria and Albert Museum, London.

away into the hands of foreigners, perhaps of enemies, the superiority we have thus laboured for and obtained! I wish to entertain a better opinion of my countrymen, than to suspect that there is a single man who could be so base; and am willing to persuade myself it has been owing to want of thought, or of proper information, that any have thus deserted the cause of their country.'

In spite of such strong appeals to his workers Wedgwood seldom objected to other manufacturers attempting the duplication of his own products. Above all, being a man of great energy and having the capacity for long hours of work, he expected similar efforts from his men. It was a discipline that laid the foundations for the industries of the nineteenth century. Having created stable production methods, Wedgwood found it necessary to expand his markets, and employ more salesmen to introduce personally his wares at home and abroad. This sales organisation reaped massive dividends, to such an extent that Wedgwood seriously undermined the business of the Meissen factory. The sale of Wedgwood wares became worldwide in the eighteenth century and with that achievement the whole ceramic industry of Great Britain came of age.

Chapter 6

English porcelain

England was not the first European country to manufacture porcelain, but, unlike many of their Continental counterparts, English porcelain manufacturers worked under highly competitive commercial conditions. The objects they produced were intended to suit the requirements and possibilities of the market in general and were not commissioned by princes and other powerful patrons. This more popular demand resulted in a vigorous commercial life, the growth of great businesses and the encouragement of talent in many fields. British manufacturers had to cater for a largely domestic market, and produced mainly everyday wares, whereas in Europe money was supplied by royal families to produce highly decorated figure models for the luxury market. In the following pages, the distinctively British style in porcelain will emerge through discussion of the main factories.

Bow 1746-1776

The factories of Bow and Chelsea can claim to be the first to have really manufactured porcelain in England in commercial quantities. Bow, however, can also claim the distinction of being the first to introduce 'bone china' to the world. The addition of animal bone ash gave added strength in the kiln during firing. Later after many further experiments with bone made by other factories, bone china became more popular.

The name of Bow is somewhat misleading for the porcelain factory was in fact situated in the parish of West Ham in Essex. In 1744 a patent was granted for the making of porcelain to Thomas Frye of West Ham and to Edward Heylyn of Bow. To date, no trace of porcelain manufactured by them has been found. It would now seem that Chelsea can claim to be the true pioneer, as a few Chelsea items bear the inscribed date 1745. It appears that Bow did not really begin commercial production until the following year. It is most likely that Frye and Heylyn took out their patent after meeting André Duché, a man

Early incised marks

Painted anchor and dagger marks, c. 1760-76

Underglaze blue mark, c. 1760-76

whose contact with William Cookworthy of Plymouth is discussed in Chapter 3.

The early output from Bow consisted entirely of tableware. The first date to be found on Bow porcelain is 1750, and the words 'New Canton' and 'Made at New Canton' also appear, referring to the place where so much Chinese porcelain was enamelled and from where it was exported. This was a period when Chinese motifs were being copied in all aspects of the visual arts.

In the 1760s production at Bow was at its height and the factory was attracting workers from other parts of the country. In the fourth edition of Daniel Defoe's *Tour of Great Britain*, published in 1748, reference is made to

'. . . Bow: where a large Manufactory of Porcelaine is lately set up. They have already made large quantities of tea-cups, saucers, etc. which by some skilful persons are said to be little inferior to those brought from China. If they can work this so as to undersell the Foreign Porcelaine, it may become a very profitable business to the Undertakers, and save great sums to the Public, which are annually sent abroad for this commodity.'

When the sixth edition of Defoe's book appeared in 1761, revised by Samuel Richardson, the entry on Bow testifies to its rapid progress:

'. . . though not as fine as some made at Chelsea, or as that from Dresden, is much stronger than either and therefore better for common use; and, being much cheaper than any other China, there is a great Demand for it. The Proprietors of this Manufactory have also procured some very good Artists in Painting, who are employed in painting some of their finest Sort of Porcelain, and is so well performed, as to equal most of that from Dresden in this Respect.'

Despite this, in 1776, after years of various controlling partnerships, the Bow manufactory was purchased and closed. Although Bow had been in business for less than thirty years its output was astonishing. The early wares were white or blue and white, closely following Oriental examples. Japanese and Chinese styles were copied and plates frequently have the Oriental type foot-rim. One feature of Bow porcelain is its thickness—even if held against a strong light, only the edges will appear translucent on many pieces. This lack of translucency is probably a result of the underfiring of the ware in an attempt to prevent it warping.

The early cream colour porcelain of this factory is subject to firing cracks, some of which may be superficial in appearance,

and may have a wax-like glaze. Later Bow tends to show something of a blue glaze, and a rust-like staining where it is worn or scratched. Many pieces of Bow are very thick and heavy for their size as a result of the paste being pressed into the mould by hand (a process known as press moulding).

Enamel colours are often used in decoration, as are powder-blue grounds. Colouring tends to be bold and puce is much used on the later figures. The first use of transfer printed decoration is found on Bow porcelain before 1760. Figure bases may also be rather tall with four Rococo scroll feet. Look out for a square hole in the back of a Bow figure: it is usually assumed that the purpose of this hole is to support a metal candle bracket if required. Again, pay careful attention to marks: early pieces are unlikely to have these although many examples have been found with several marks associated with the Bow factory (for example a dagger, a longbow, or an anchor) on the one item.

Bristol 1770-1781

William Cookworthy established his hard-paste factory in Bristol in 1770 after its removal from Plymouth. Five

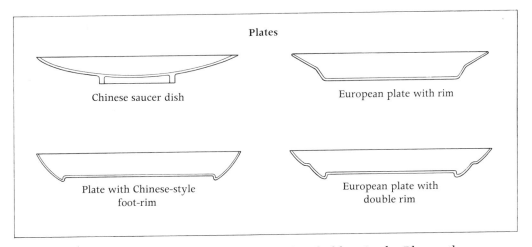

Plates

Chinese saucer dish

European plate with rim

Plate with Chinese-style
foot-rim

European plate with
double rim

Painted 'X' or 'B' mark

Crossed-swords mark,
1770-81

Bristolians had been shareholders in the Plymouth company, including the famous Richard Champion who was to take control at Bristol. Champion, like Cookworthy, was a Quaker; he was also a merchant and a Whig. When Cookworthy retired, Champion became increasingly involved with the production of porcelain. In 1775 he applied to extend the patent that had given Cookworthy 'sole use and exercise of a discovery of materials of the same nature as those of which Asiatic and Dresden porcelain are made'. His plans were frustrated by the Staffordshire potters and in particular by Josiah Wedgwood, who knew that the china clay was the finest available and who also had more money. An expensive case resulted that lasted months and at the end of it the Bristol monopoly no longer existed, and Josiah Wedgwood had access to the Cornish clay he so badly needed for his pottery. This, together with problems of administration and disputes with former colleagues,

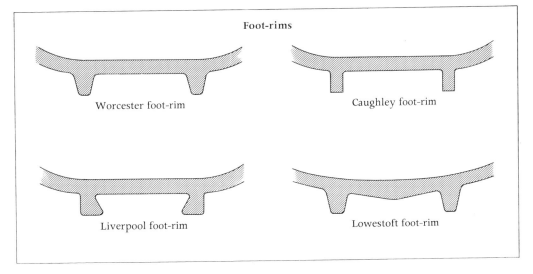

Foot-rims

Worcester foot-rim

Caughley foot-rim

Liverpool foot-rim

Lowestoft foot-rim

meant that costs proved too much and the Bristol factory finished its short life in 1781. Seven years later Champion died at the age of forty-eight.

Bristol porcelain is of very high quality and the domestic porcelains were expensive. It has the finest gilding of all the English factories. Floral garlands are typical and the Rococo style is most favoured. The commissioned wares, however, are in a class of their own. Many good models, most of them human figures, were produced at Bristol. Rarely see now are the biscuit ware plaques, with flowers surrounding a bust, monogram or animal. These originally cost £5 each and were mostly made for presentation.

Caughley 1772-1814

Thomas Turner probably trained at Worcester and after moving to Caughley he went into partnership with Ambrose Gallimore who had a pottery next to a coalmine. After the pottery had been enlarged it was renamed the Salopian Porcelain Manufactory: the name Salopia comes from the Roman name for Shropshire in which Caughley is situated. Porcelain manufacture began by about 1775 although pottery is believed to have been made there from 1754. The fact that so much of Caughley (pronounced 'Calflee') resembles Worcester is no doubt explained by Turner's connection with that factory. The porcelain tends to be slightly more heavily potted (having a thicker, less refined appearance) than Worcester although similar in other ways.

In 1799 the lease of the Caughley factory was sold to John Rose whose factory was at Coalport on the other bank of the

SALOPIAN

Impressed name-mark, *c.* 1775-99

S So Sx

Painted or printed 'S' marks, *c.* 1775-*c.* 1795

Printed and painted 'C' mark, *c.* 1775-95

river and, for a time, he continued to use the Caughley site for some of his Coalport production.

Most of Caughley products were tea wares and the last factory sale of surplus stock included:
'. . . a great number of beautiful tea and coffee equipages of various much improved patterns, in full and short sets, richly executed in enamel and burnished gold together with a great variety of new and elegant blue and white tea and coffee sets, table and dessert services, muffin plates, butter tubs etc., mugs, jugs, egg-cups and strainers, butter cups, custard cups of different sorts and sizes, pickle-shells, eye baths, asparagus servers, toy table and tea sets and candle-sticks etc . . .'

The output was largely blue-and-white and in the Oriental or 'Nankin' style. 'Nankin' described much blue-and-white, for it was the main centre of the vast export of such wares by the Chinese, just as most Chinese enamelled wares were exported through Canton.

Caughley was regarded by generations of collectors as a poor cousin to the Worcester factory, only 30 miles (48 km) away on the River Severn. Now excavation has proved this attitude to be totally misinformed, as we shall see later. It was Mr Geoffrey Godden who, after investigating the Caughley site, made several major discoveries concerning the wares and their marks, and this table will clarify the differences revealed between Caughley and Worcester as a result.

	Caughley	Worcester
The Fisherman Pattern	The fisherman holds the rod with a taut line.	Fisherman holds rod with very loose fishing line.
	Standing fisherman holds a short fat fish.	Standing fisherman on boat holds a long thin fish.
	The inner border is filled with solid pigment.	The inner border is composed of engraved lines.
Disguised Numeral Marks	No marks of this type revealed by excavation, although formerly attributed to this factory. Thus Caughley is much rarer than originally believed.	Marks (nine) formerly attributed to Caughley now regarded as Worcester.
Moulded Cabbage-Leaf Jugs	The eyes are open but the eyelids are thicker. In other ways the jugs are similar to the Worcester variety.	The eyes are of the Oriental type and appear to be closed.

The porcelain characteristics of both factories are very similar when held under a light bulb: green for early examples, orange for the later ones. This suggests that both factories purchased their raw materials from the same source.

Chelsea

Among the eighteenth-century English porcelains it is only Chelsea that may be ranked with the great wares of the royal factories of France and Germany. English manufacturers did not enjoy patronage on the scale of their Continental counterparts, so the production of luxury items, the marvellous figure models and great vases, was the exception, not the rule. Chelsea, in contrast to other English factories, deliberately catered for the luxury trade.

Remarkably, Chelsea's guiding light was Nicholas Sprimont (1716-1771), a Huguenot silversmith who registered his mark at Goldsmith's Hall in 1742. Several porcelains were experimented with at Chelsea, and numerous differences can be observed among the characteristics of most mixed groups of Chelsea available. In order to clarify its development, Chelsea is usually divided into periods defined by its mark changes:

The Triangle Period. This early period, in the first half of the eighteenth century, is rare. The mark is a triangle incised into

Early triangle marks, occasionally accompanied by the place-name

Underglaze blue crown and trident mark, *c.* 1748-50

116

102 A cream 'goat and bee' jug, relief-moulded and painted. Marked with an incised triangle. Height 4½ inches (114 mm). Chelsea, mid eighteenth century. Victoria and Albert Museum, London.

Raised anchor mark, c. 1749-52

103 Below: Leaf-moulded teapot painted with flowers and insects. Chelsea, mid eighteenth century.

104 Far right: The same teapot from below, showing the incised triangle.

the paste before glazing, which accounts for its rarity: triangle marks are unusual and some marks have been cut through the glaze at a much later date in the hope that they might be mistaken for an early piece. Some of these pieces are also incised with the date 1745 and 'goat and bee jugs' are good examples of this. These translucent little jugs are a delight with a figure of a bee among the foliage and a goat's head cut into the base. The porcelain has a yellowish tinge and the glaze is often a little cloudy.

In my experience it is the white porcelains that are most often overlooked. During the 1960s a dealer I knew purchased a 'goat and bee jug' as part of an auction lot of miscellaneous white kitchen ware! Most of the output before 1750 was white and designs are often based on contemporary silver shapes.

The Raised-Anchor Period 1749-1752. At this period the now famous Chelsea anchor was moulded in relief on a raised pad. Figure models with this mark are of the highest standard and the white figures of the birds made at this time are outstanding among European porcelains; needless to say they can also be costly. Tin oxide was added to the glaze and can usually be detected wherever the glaze gathers and pools, as it has an opaque milky appearance and is not translucent. Bone ash was also used to help strengthen the porcelain body. When these early pieces are held against a strong light they usually reveal the light patches or pinpoints of extra translucency that are termed 'moons'.

It is at this time that we also see the delightful 'fable painted' wares of J. H. O'Neale. Many octagonal tea wares were decorated by O'Neale, and some of the designs were taken from Aesop.

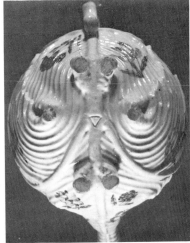

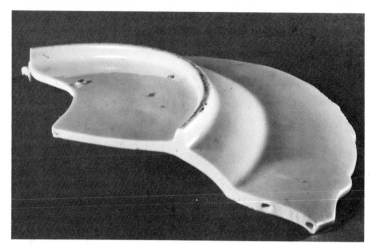

105 A broken Chelsea plate clearly showing that the 'moons', a well-known Chelsea characteristic, are in fact the result of air pockets or bubbles of varying size. (For a long time they were believed to be the result of glassy areas in the paste.) The 'stilt marks' and the tiny red anchor marks are also visible.

The Red Anchor Period 1752-1756. The red anchor was applied at this period almost as though the manufacturer intended it to be invisible! The anchor is very small and I have seen marked examples that have been in a private collection for many years without the collector ever seeing the marks until they were pointed out to him. It was occasionally applied in brown, though mostly on flat wares.

Red anchor mark, c. 1752-56

'Stilt marks', small raised patches, may be found on the reverse of plates and dishes showing where they were supported in the kiln by stilts. Again, small characteristics such as these are most important, for so many of these porcelains bear no factory mark at all. Attention to the marks is all the more important as only they make it possible to separate many of the raised anchor and red anchor pieces, which often have the same milky glaze and crazing.

O'Neale carried out much of his best painting at this period. Vegetable-shaped tureens are distinctive, as too is the use of botanical subjects as decoration. Hans Sloane plates are well-known examples, copied from illustrations in the *Gardener's dictionary* by Philip Miller published under the aegis of Sir Hans Sloane, patron of the Royal Physik Garden, Chelsea, as are drawings from Curtis' botanical works. Figures were sometimes inspired by Kändler's original Meissen models. Classical and emblematic figures were made in quantity. Leaf-shapes were used quite often for sauceboats and dishes. Painted insects or flowers were often used to conceal small faults in the glaze. An object of truly great artistry is the red anchor group of Leda and the Swan painted in enamels.

The Gold Anchor Period 1756-1769. This period is distinguished by the use of a small gold anchor. The porcelain is thick and contains bone ash although there is no longer tin

Gold anchor mark, c. 1756-69

118

oxide in the glaze. The Scotsman John Donaldson, who was influenced by Continental painters, did good figure painting. Some major figure groups, such as 'The Music Lesson', exemplify the overwhelming use of floral bocage decoration at this time. Miniature objects or toys were manufactured, some of them copied from Meissen. Seals and scent bottles proved very popular and have remained so with today's collectors.

Chelsea/Derby Period

Chelsea production came to an end when Nicholas Sprimont sold out to John Cox, who in 1770 promptly sold the Chelsea factory to William Duesbury of Derby. Around this period it becomes very difficult to tell the difference between the products of the two factories.

Double or linked gold anchor marks point to the Chelsea/ Derby period, as do ones crossed or combined with a 'D'. It could well be, however, that many pieces marked in this way were made at Derby rather than Chelsea. As with Derby figures, unglazed patch marks often occur on the base. This is a vital characteristic which the collector should bear in mind when identifying these factories as these rarely occur on work from other factories.

Gold (or occasionally red) mark

Gold mark

Coalport 1796 – present day

The early wares of Coalport are unmarked and often mistaken for Chamberlain Worcester because of the similar decoration. The later Coalport work marked with the date 1750 also gives many a headache to new collectors: the date merely refers to the assumed beginning of the Caughley factory which John Rose purchased in 1799.

Coalport produced porcelain of outstanding quality, and their leadless felspathic glaze (created from ground felspar suspended in water) obtained the Award of the Society of Arts on 30 May 1820. This award was celebrated by Coalport with a handsome special mark.

Coalport marks
1. Impressed mark, 1085-25
2. Early painted mark, c. 1805-15
3. Marks painted in underglaze blue, c. 1810-25
4. Printed mark introduced after Society of Arts Gold Metal award, c. 1820-30
5. Painted or gilt monogram mark, c. 1851-61
6. Mark in enamels or gold, c. 1851-61
7. Painted or gilt 'ampersand' mark, c. 1861-75

In terms of translucency and whiteness, Coalport rivalled the products of Swansea and Nantgarw. In 1816 a newspaper went so far as to state:

'The Sèvres China Manufacture has now competitors which bid fair to excel in the Article of China. The Manufactories at Coalbrookdale and at Swansea having just completed some beautiful specimens.'

Rose was a businessman as well as potter, for he signed a seven-year agreement with the brilliant *enfant terrible* of English ceramics, William Billingsley, so stifling the competition from the Welsh factories.

Coalport was, and continues to be, highly regarded for its production of vases and other wares decorated with various flower motifs. As with Caughley, however, there was much upheaval in estimation of the value of Coalport when Geoffrey Godden discovered pattern books at Minton that proved that many pieces always thought to be Coalport or Coalbrookdale were in fact from that factory.

The gilding on Coalport porcelain is rich and thick, the painting is always excellent, and the pieces decorated with Sèvres type coloured grounds are quite beautiful.

H. & R. Daniel *c.* 1822–1845

Henry Daniel produced highly competitive porcelain in Stoke-on-Trent, although marked pieces are not easy to find. Daniel had been chief enameller to Spode, and he was joined in the business by his son Richard.

The reputation of this firm's porcelains was held in the highest esteem by the manufacturers, yet it is only during the second half of the 1970s that its products have begun to receive the attention from collectors that they deserve. It is thus yet

106 *Above:* Floral encrusted pastille burner in the form of a cottage. Coalport, 1820.

107 *Opposite:* The so-called 'Maypole Dancers', a rare and exuberant Chelsea group, 1755. Fitzwilliam Museum, Cambridge.

DANIEL & SON
Rare mark, *c.* 1822–26

H. & R. DANIEL
Rare written or printed mark, *c.* 1826–29

108 Painted plate, teapot and documentary bowl. Coalport, early nineteenth century.

109 *Opposite, top:* Bow porcelain figures. The broken specimen reveals the thickness of the porcelain which is a result of the paste being hand-pressed into the moulds, and which makes the figure heavy to handle. Note also the square hole in the base of the broken figure—another Bow characteristic.

110 *Opposite, bottom:* A typical Chelsea tureen in the form of a hare. Red anchor period, 1755. Victoria and Albert Museum, London.

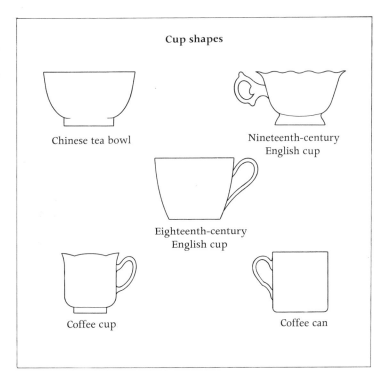

Cup shapes

Chinese tea bowl

Nineteenth-century English cup

Eighteenth-century English cup

Coffee cup

Coffee can

another example of how objects of quality can be completely overlooked until attention is drawn to them.

While Daniel porcelain is subject to cracks during firing and crazing in the glaze is often present in the finished article, the experience their maker gained while decorating for Spode makes these porcelains, with their shaped edges, most desirable.

Standard early impressed mark

Standard printed mark, *c.* 1805-20

Overglaze printed mark, *c.* 1815-30

Davenport *c.* 1793-1887

John Davenport began his family business at Longport, Staffordshire, although at first only earthenware was produced. The quality of the nineteenth-century Davenport pieces was very high, although I am certain that many of their productions, as with Daniel and Coalport, were once classified as 'Rockingham'. Rockingham was a general term for anything Victorian considered to be quality, although as a factory its production is now known to be much smaller than once thought. This arbitrary classification was applied to much nineteenth-century porcelain due to the refusal to believe that so much outstanding work could have emanated from the Victorian era. This firm was also responsible for excellent transfer-printed earthenware, but despite this the business failed in 1887.

123

The output of the Davenport concern was a large one, particularly in the field of tea and dessert services, and some excellent artists worked for the firm. Many of the Derby porcelains were copied as were those of Spode. As with Coalport, a *rose Pompadour* ground was used. At the same time the cheaper market was catered for with the production of 'opaque semi-porcelain' which simply meant an improved earthenware.

DAVENPORT
LONGPORT
STAFFORDSHRE

Standard printed mark, *c.* 1870-87

Derby *c.* 1750-present day

The name Derby is renowned both as a city and as a porcelain manufactory where porcelain of great variety has been produced for more than 200 years. The term is confusing to many because of the changes of ownership, and because many new collectors tend to refer to all Derby wares as Royal Crown Derby no matter what their age. The Royal Crown Derby Porcelain Company Limited takes its name from the time it received a royal warrant in 1889; for objects made before that date other terms need to be used.

Incised or painted mark, *c.* 1760-80 (?)

Standard mark, 1782-1818

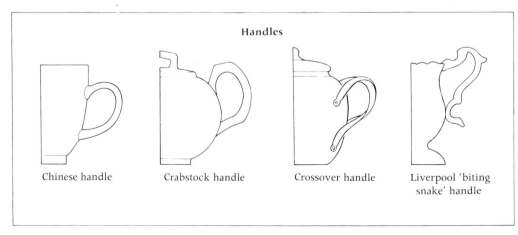

Handles

Chinese handle   Crabstock handle   Crossover handle   Liverpool 'biting snake' handle

112 A charming eighteenth-century Derby figure group.

Later standard mark in red, more carelessly drawn

Transfer-printed mark, 1818-48

King Street Factory mark

Derby came into being largely as a result of the business management and talent for porcelain decoration of William Duesbury. It was Duesbury who agreed at the beginning of 1756 to be co-patron with John Heath, described as a Gentleman, and André Planché, china maker. They set out to work together '. . . in the art of making English china as also in buying and selling of all sorts of wares belonging to the art of making china . . .' Planché was a French refugee who probably began the first porcelain production in Derby some years earlier than 1756. At this time William Duesbury was in London with his own decorating shop, painting wares from Bow, Chelsea, Derbyshire and Staffordshire. In due course Duesbury was left in control of the factory.

Duesbury copied many Chelsea products as well as originals from Meissen. Some of the early figures from Derby have an unglazed edge around the base, known as a 'dry edge', others have a somewhat narrow funnel-shaped hole underneath. The later figures have the 'patch marks' on the base mentioned in the section on Chelsea. Three and sometimes four patch marks, about the size of a thumb print, were created by the small clay pads used to support the figures and these prevented the glaze

125

sticking during firing. Model numbers are also frequently incised in the bases of figures. Gilding is also a feature of Derby, and both honey and mercurial gilding is much admired.

Due to the popularity of the bisque figures being created by Sèvres, Derby began the production of undecorated biscuit figures from about 1770. Only perfect figures were left in the biscuit, or unglazed, state; those having imperfections were sold off cheaply having first been glazed and decorated.

Many famous decorators worked for Derby, but the most celebrated was William Billingsley (1758-1828). After serving his apprenticeship, Billingsley became Derby's principal flower painter in 1790. This complex man was later to move from factory to factory, ever searching for the elusive perfect porcelain formula. Even so, most people take delight in Billingsley for his painting of flowers and roses in particular. He was a naturalistic flower painter, who, having first washed the whole flower with colour, then removed the highlights with a dry brush, before painting in such detail as shading. The 'Billingsley Rose' is unmistakeable.

113 The base of the group shown on page 125, revealing such useful points of identification as the hole, unglazed areas usually described as 'pad' or 'patch' marks caused by the pads of clay used to support the figure while in the kiln, and the incised number, another typical feature of later Derby figures.

Billingsley was succeeded at Derby by William Pegg, known more familiarly as 'Quaker' Pegg. Outstanding in the botanical field, Pegg's style was to paint his flowers across the entire width of the piece he was decorating. In 1800 he joined the Society of Friends and developed a form of religious mania. He first rejected his botanical painting in the belief that he was creating idols. After many years he returned to Derby and his painting in 1813, but in 1820 the mania returned and he left for the last time.

A brief chronology of Derby may be given as follows:

1750-1756 First figures made at Derby by André Planché.

1756 William Duesbury senior becomes manager.

1786 Death of Duesbury senior, succeeded by his son William Duesbury junior.

1795 Michael Kean taken into partnership.

1797 Kean becomes manager on the death of Duesbury junior.

1815 Robert Bloor takes over from the Duesbury family.

1848 The old Nottingham Road factory is closed and a small factory started in King Street, Derby, by workmen from the old works.

1878 Formation of the Derby Crown Porcelain Company in Osmeston Road.

1890 Name of factory changed to Royal Crown Derby Porcelain Company.

1935 King Street factory merged with the Royal Crown Derby Porcelain Company.

1964 Royal Crown Derby Porcelain Company became part of the Allied English Potteries Group.

Doulton 1882-present day

The porcelains made at Burslem at the Nile Street works in this century are widely known and form a highly collectable series. In particular some beautiful effects have been achieved with rich flambé glazes.

However, it is for the production of stonewares that Doulton is most celebrated, of which more in the following chapter. From the early 1880s some excellent porcelains have been made. From the final years of the Victorian era until the eve of the First World War, pieces of great technical interest and representative of their times were produced. Much interest is now being taken in such pieces for, after some neglect, they were made long enough ago to be seen in their proper perspective. Usually an 'all over' painting technique was employed and the examples of particular note are ones signed by the artist.

Bases

Derby base

Bow base

Chelsea base

Obadiah Sherratt table base

127

Teapot shapes

Yi-hsing ware teapot

Eighteenth-century globular teapot

Pinxton teapot, late eighteenth century

Caughley teapot, late eighteenth century

New Hall teapots, early nineteenth century

Castleford teapot

Rockingham 'Cadogan' teapot

'Barge' teapot

Coalport teapot, *c.* 1825

Victorian teapot

Goss *c.* 1858-1940

W. H. GOSS

Impressed or printed mark, *c.* 1858 +

W.H.COSS.

Printed crest mark

The reputation of Goss has suffered severely after the great mass of heraldic or crested china that first appeared on the souvenir market during the 1880s. In the first twenty years of this century the collection of such pieces became a craze and their output was very large. Even so, interest in some of these pieces, particularly the figures, houses, cottages, ships and vehicles, has revived among modern collectors. Such items will never rank with those of the great porcelain factories, but they clearly provide pleasure for many.

William Henry Goss (1833-1906) first worked as an artist at a firm known as Copelands (see the section on Spode), and his early parian busts, his 'porcelain jewellery', 'jewelled porcelain' and pastille-burners in the form of cottage models are of real note. Pre-First World War pieces attract most attention: the modelling is often very good and some pieces display a true sense of humour and are genuine curiosities.

Liverpool

Painted monogram, rare, 18th century

In the past collectors have talked of Liverpool porcelain as though it was the product of one factory, although this is in fact not the case.

Eighteenth-century Liverpool was well placed to be a centre of English ceramics. It was an excellent port, and it was also well served by the Trent and Mersey canal which brought cargoes of pottery from Staffordshire. Furthermore, it was the base of Sadler and Green who ran a transfer printing business catering for creamwares and porcelains alike. As we have seen earlier, Liverpool was also the home of a number of potteries producing tin glazed Delftwares.

Various pastes were used by different porcelain manufacturers, but the main decorative output was of Oriental style blue-and-white. Like most of the English porcelains the Liverpool products were made for everyday use rather than pure ornament.

A whole colony of potters grew up at Shaws Brow on Merseyside. The largest among them was probably Richard Chaffers & Co (*fl. c.* 1754-65). First established as a pottery before 1750, this company began the manufacture of soapstone type porcelain about 1756. The soaprock used was obtained from Cornwall and enamelled decoration was used as well as underglaze blue, but again, it is the Oriental styles that prevail. The body of this porcelain is somewhat grey and the glaze

occasionally gathers within the foot-rims to form a rather dirty discolouration that is frequently termed a 'thunder-cloud effect'.

Many of the Liverpool soapstone porcelains are inferior to those of Worcester but there are frequent exceptions where the potting is thin and crisp, closely resembling Worcester.

The Chaffers factory, like most Liverpool factories, produced jugs with a rather elongated appearance. Philip Christian, who took over after Richard Chaffers's death in 1765, produced pots of rather more elegance including some charming enamelled coffee pots with moulded well placed spouts and lively and well shaped handles. The Philip Christian factory continued until 1776, the year in which he sold his lease of a Cornish soapstone mine to Worcester.

Samuel Gillbody (*fl. c.* 1754-61) was responsible for at least some of the exceedingly rare Liverpool porcelain figures. His modelling and painting has a precise charm about it. There is an enamelled figure of Minerva to be seen in the Victoria and Albert Museum, London.

Soapstone bodied wares are attributed to William Ball (*fl. c.* 1755-69). His blues tend to be bright and the clear, and the soft glaze has a warm feel about it. The painting usually consists of firmly executed chinoiseries.

The porcelain body from the factory of William Reid & Co. (*c.* 1755-1761) is thick and distinctive, rather like the early pipe clays, and the addition of tin oxide to the glaze gives it a dense and bubbled appearance. There is still much to be learned about these porcelains from excavation, however, and there

114 *Far left:* A very fine example of a moulded and blue painted porcelain mug. Liverpool, eighteenth century.

115 *Above:* Herculaneum plate, part of a service decorated with the arms of the City of Liverpool. Early nineteenth century.

may be yet more re-attribution of Liverpool porcelains.

The Penningtons were an important family of Liverpool potters and formed a company known as Pennington & Part (c. 1770-1799). The bone-ash bodies believed to be by this factory are often decorated with prints in underglaze blue but they are poor in comparison with Worcester or Caughley.

The body used at the factory of Thomas Wolfe & Co. (c. 1795-1800) is of a harder paste and some of its products are not unlike those of New Hall. The translucency shows a greenish tinge. A number of the Liverpool porcelains have printed decoration, and those used at the Ball factory were frequently overpainted in enamels. Finials on Liverpool teapot lids often seem unusually high and handles in the form of a biting snake – where the snake appears to be biting the rim of the pot – are a firm help in identification.

The name of the Herculaneum factory (c. 1793-1841) was chosen out of the same motives that led Wedgwood to call his great factory Etruria. Herculaneum was one of the first factories in England to produce a non-frit bone china, although its first wares were entirely earthenware. The creamwares and stonewares frequently carry the impressed mark 'Herculaneum' and are of a fine standard. Blue transfer-printed earthenware was also produced but the porcelain is of great interest and was much overlooked in the past. Particularly important are vase decorations in the French Empire style but with very English enamelled reserves.

Longton Hall 1749-1760

Rare early marks, painted in underglaze blue

This was the first porcelain factory to appear in the Potteries and is situated near Stoke-on-Trent. It was founded by William Jenkinson, and the first products show the influence of salt-glaze pottery.

Jenkinson was followed by a number of partners, one of whom was William Littler who gave his name to the bright blue used at Longton, called 'Littler's Blue'. Littler is said to have been the first potter to introduce cobalt blue into the Potteries.

The porcelain body is heavy and often clumsy, a soft paste glassy frit, but it is much admired by many collectors. Many soft pastes have more charm than the technically perfect hard pastes, but this is very much a matter of personal opinion.

The surface of many examples is uneven and the thick glaze has a candle-wax appearance. Most characteristic of the Longton wares are the leaf-shaped examples with the veins of the leaves often outlined in pink.

Some good painting was done at Longton, and a series of white porcelain figures, representing animals, characters from classical mythology and models based on Meissen originals, are known as 'the snowmen group'. The glaze of these pieces is thick, bubbly and glassy while the paste is subject to fire cracks.

116 Longton Hall two-handled sauceboat and two dishes. They show the leaf-moulding so characteristic of this factory and the heaviness of the porcelain. Mid eighteenth century.

Lowestoft 1757-1799

A fishing port on the coast of Suffolk, Lowestoft has long been a celebrated name among porcelain collectors. With no more than thirty workers, it was probably the smallest porcelain factory in England; it was also the best example of a soft paste one. It catered mainly for local needs and even after twenty years of production the business was still being described as "China Manufacturers and Herring Curers". It sold well to the middle-class population of East Anglia, as well as supplying a stream of souvenirs for the eighteenth-century tourist.

135

Rare painter's numbers, in underglaze blue, c. 1760-75

Copies of blue Worcester crescent and Dresden crossed-swords, c. 1775-90

One visitor, a man named Thomas Wale, made the following entry in his diary in 1777: 'Drove down with Mr. Smith and two sons to Lowestoft where we saw the china ware fabric, etc. and all of us bought some of it. Saw ye hanging gardens and ye fine prospect of ye sea. Excellent bathing machines etc.'

Views of Lowestoft and portraits of ships formed ready subjects for the Lowestoft decorators, who also copied the Oriental wares that had such popularity.

The factory closed by 1800, and although production was

considerable, examples of Lowestoft are not easy to find. They attract the collector for two reasons: their simple charm that results from the Chinese designs and the fact that such products as eye-baths, ink pots, and birth tablets recording the name and date of birth of local children, are appealing in their homeliness.

Flat bases are glazed over, and on wares with foot-rims, painters' numbers are to be found on the inside of the rim. The most famous products of this factory are those marked 'A Trifle From Lowestoft'.

Lowestoft wares are thick and have a thick bubbled glaze. Enamel colours were used after 1770, sometimes in conjunction with underglaze blue borders. Early specimens often have relief moulded decoration with reserve panels in underglaze blue. Of the enamel patterns, the bold floral sprays applied to tea and coffee wares, with a prominent tulip, are very fine. A few rare figures were also made at Lowestoft.

Minton c. 1793-present day

Thomas Minton was born in 1765 and began his career as a potter when he was apprenticed to Thomas Turner at Caughley. In Shropshire he learned the skills of engraving copper plates for the production of blue printed ware, and he would also have met Robert Hancock, the leading exponent of ceramic engraving. It proved an ideal environment for such an intelligent young man. When his apprenticeship was over Minton stayed briefly at Caughley before going up to London where he is said to have engraved work for Josiah Spode.

Following his marriage in London, Minton moved to Stoke-on-Trent and established himself in business as a designer and engraver. He then decided that he must have his own pottery

117 *Below:* Two Lowestoft mugs of the late eighteenth century.

118 *Far right:* Floral encrusted two-handled porcelain bowl and cover. Minton, nineteenth century. Crossed-swords mark on the base in underglaze blue. Such pieces were in the past frequently thought to be either Meissen or Coalport.

and, as Simeon Shaw in his *History of the Staffordshire Potteries* describes:

'About 1793 Mr. Thomas Minton connected himself with a Mr. Pownall and Joseph Poulson, and at Stoke commenced the manufacture of Blue Printed Pottery, of much excellence of quality and with additional elegance of Pattern, which speedily secured considerable celebrity. A few years afterwards, the manufacture of porcelain was connected with the other and has been attended with success. The manufactory is now the property of Mr. Minton alone. The Porcelain there fabricated possesses great excellence for fine texture and elegant ornaments . . .'

It appears that the years of Minton's production of porcelain are 1797 to 1816 and after 1824. It was during the latter period that a large number of decorative wares were made by Minton which in later years, as records were overlooked, became attributed to many other factories such as Derby, Rockingham, Spode, Swansea, Worcester and Coalport. This designation was corrected by a discovery made in the late 1960s by Geoffrey Godden, author and china expert. Researching the Minton archives he found design books that proved Minton's production of wares previously unsuspected. 'It was', he wrote, 'as if a new factory had been discovered.' Mr Godden tells the story in full in his book *Minton Pottery and Porcelain of the First Period 1793-1850*.

Minton travelled to Cornwall in 1798 and 1799 with other major potters in an attempt to stabilise the cost of china clay. When he died in 1836 he was succeeded by his son Herbert, an outstanding figure in the history of the Potteries in the nineteenth century. He attracted the finest decorators in Britain and some of the most notable from the Continent. Herbert Minton gained an international reputation for his company as well as royal patronage, and at the Great Exhibition in 1851 his ceramic innovations and displays won wide acclaim. We shall examine some of the nineteenth-century productions of Minton in more detail in the next chapter.

New Hall 1782-*c.* 1835

The patents of the Bristol factory were sold by Richard Champion in 1781 to a new company in the Potteries. The factory was first at Tunstall before moving to Shelton Hall, later known as New Hall. Production consisted chiefly of utility wares, particularly tea wares of all kinds. The decoration consists largely of small floral sprays, and larger bunches

1. Painted mark in overglaze blue enamel, *c.* 1805-16
2. Dresden crossed-swords mark, 1820s

3. Incised mark, *c.* 1845-60
4. Painted or printed ermine device, *c.* 1850-70

MINTON   MINTONS

Impressed name-mark, 1862+

L. Solon
or
M. L. Solon

Artist's signature

1. Painted pattern number, *c.* 1781-1812
2. Printed mark, *c.* 1812-35

119 Shapes and decoration typical of the New Hall factory. Note the coffee pot with its unusual stand, and the teapot with its floreat-like feet shown in the top left of the photograph, a feature only found on early examples.

and baskets of flowers, and at times a distinctive yellow shell. Gilding is often of good quality and Oriental mandarin patterns were also produced. After 1810 the porcelain body changed from the Bristol formula to bone ash. Tablewares are often banded round the base and printed outlines are sometimes enamelled. The early hard paste pieces are seldom marked with more than a pattern number, and those bearing the factory name are usually from the bone china period.

Pinxton 1796-1813

John Coke (1776-1841), having become interested in the porcelain factory at Meissen on a tour of France, returned to his estate at Pinxton, on the borders of Nottinghamshire and Derbyshire; there he noticed some interesting clays and wrote to William Duesbury about them.

Duesbury was apparently not interested, but the news reached the ears of William Billingsley and he was immediately enthusiastic. He persuaded Coke to build a factory and told him that he would like to become works manager. The first porcelain was fired in April 1796 and Billingsley moved from Derby to Pinxton late in the autumn of that year.

Rare painted or gilt name-mark, c. 1796-1805

1 P_{108} 2 $\ast$)

1. Rare painted initial, with pattern number
2. Painted crescent and star mark

Unfortunately there were no profits to pay Billingsley and he left Pinxton to go to Mansfield. His place was taken by William Caffee, also from Derby. In 1806 John Coke leased the factory to John Cutts but when Cutts moved to Wedgwood in 1813, the factory at Pinxton was closed.

The main Pinxton decoration consists of landscapes and flowers. The early Pinxton resembled the Derby body and has a green translucency when held in front of a bulb. Billingsley no doubt saw Pinxton as a heaven-sent opportunity to attempt to perfect his own porcelain body. At this time Pinxton closely resembles the bodies used by Billingsley in Wales at Swansea and Nantgarw. It is thinly potted and highly translucent. Under John Cutts the body thickened again and the translucency becomes yellowish.

120 Sugar box (centre), tea cup and saucer (right) and coffee can and saucer (left), all showing the fine painting and high quality porcelain associated with Pinxton.

Plymouth 1768-1773

This was the first English factory to use hard paste and it is curious to note how closely the Plymouth figures resemble the soft paste productions of Bow and Longton Hall.

It was William Cookworthy who opened the factory, and although supported by Lord Camelford it became clear even after two years' production and considerable expenditure on the part of both men that the factory was unlikely to become a financial success. The real difficulty arose in achieving a consistent paste, as Lord Camelford was to write in 1790: 'The difficulties found in proportioning properly the ingredients so as to give exactly the necessary degree of vitrification and no more, and the niceties with regard to this manipulation discouraged us from proceeding with the concern after we had procured the patent for the material

Painted marks in underglaze blue or enamels, c. 1768-70

Impressed mark

136

and expended on it between two and three thousand pounds.'

Some of the early figures were left undecorated, which made the flaws in the porcelain after firing very visible. Tall, hexagonal, broad-shouldered vases are typical but glazes were often discoloured during the firing. Resemblance to Bow and Longton Hall is found in the shell pieces, which consist of either a simple scallop shape or more than one shell joined together, and in the fact that some Longton Hall moulds were bought by Cookworthy in 1760. There are fine bell-shape mugs, sometimes showing 'wreathing' or faint spiral markings in the paste that can be felt with the fingers. Some of the later Plymouth vases are often beautifully painted.

Ridgway *c.* 1808-1855

The Ridgway family were all considerable potters but in the field of porcelain it is John Ridgway who particularly interests us. His father, Job Ridgway, had returned to Hanley in 1781 after working in Swansea and Leeds, and five years later his son John was born. The Cauldon Place Works at Shelton was built in 1802 and it was here that John, together with his younger brother William, joined their father in partnership in 1808. The same year they began the manufacture of porcelain. The best period, however, is regarded as being from 1813 until 1830 when the bone china body is heavy, with a clear paste and a clear glaze.

John Ridgway's main output was of tea and dessert wares, often richly decorated.

Rockingham *c.* 1826-1842

Printed griffin mark, *c.* 1826-30

This short-lived but much attributed factory takes its name from Earl Fitzwilliam, Marquis of Rockingham, on whose Yorkshire estate the factory was built. The potters here were the Brameld family, and the sons, Frederick, George and Thomas, managed the factory during the years of porcelain production.

The Rockingham bone china type body appears softer than other bone china of the time, which perhaps explains the tendency of the glaze to craze. Shapes used by Rockingham are very characteristic and a feel for them is easily obtained after a little study, and the same can be said of the colours (green, puce, grey). There is also some excellent landscape painting in the reserves (the areas left free of background decoration).

137

121 *Left*: Part of a rather florid tea service with relief decoration. Rockingham, *c.* 1835.

122 *Right*: Coalport pot-pourri vase and cover of typical high quality and with floral decoration. It was described as a 'new poperee vase' in the Coalport *Traveller's Design Book* and sold originally for three guineas, then a considerable sum of money. Height $11\frac{1}{2}$ inches (292 mm), *c.* 1830–35. Victoria and Albert Museum, London.

Some figures were made as were models of cottages and castles. Dessert services are of high quality, such as the one made for William IV in 1830, but it is a fortunate collector who finds one complete. The decorative style favoured at Rockingham was the Rococo, with plenty of scrolls and applied flowers.

Spode 1770-present day

Spode was not producing porcelain until the 1790s in the time of Josiah Spode junior, who was responsible for an excellent body. Under his brilliant direction the Spode factory and its products became known throughout the world.

The first Josiah Spode (born in 1739) had, when he was sixteen years old, worked with Whieldon and once again we see how this great potter was able to fire the enthusiasm of his young workers and stimulate their work.

In 1970 one of the most remarkable exhibitions of the ceramics of one manufactory was held in London, at the Royal

Spode marks

1. Impressed mark, *c.* 1770
2. Painted mark, *c.* 1800
3. Impressed mark, *c.* 1800
4. Painted mark, *c.* 1812
5. Printed mark, *c.* 1833
6. Impressed mark, *c.* 1833
7. Printed mark, *c.* 1850
8. Printed mark, *c.* 1855
9. Printed mark, *c.* 1894
10. Printed mark, *c.* 1970

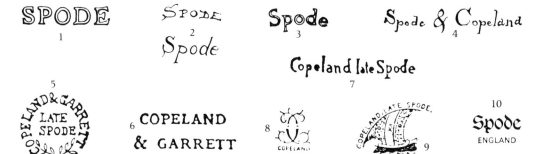

138

123 *Right:* White porcelain
figure of a goat. Plymouth,
c. 1768. British Museum,
London.

124 *Below:* A Rockingham
porcelain basket painted
with a view of Brighton. It
shows Brighton's first pier
with its chain construction.
There is a griffin mark on the
base.

125 Part of a bone china tea service. Spode, 1850.

Academy of Arts at Burlington House: it celebrated '200 years of Spode'. The catalogue of that exhibition, which was remarkable in its range and quality, is itself an excellent introduction to Spode.

In 1813 Spode introduced a stone-china body so that replacements could be made to china trade porcelain. It was a time of many innovations and improvements. The rich decoration of the porcelain was carried out in a separate decorating establishment in the Spode factory that was owned and managed by Daniel. This unique arrangement was terminated in the summer of 1822, Daniel establishing his own factory in Stoke.

A felspar porcelain was introduced in 1821, and this fact is commemorated in the factory mark.

The Copeland family had long been associated with Spode, and in March 1833 a partnership of Copeland and Garrett succeeded him. They began to market their new statuary porcelain, or 'parian', in the early 1840s.

Copeland and Garrett were succeeded by Messrs W. T. Copeland. A considerable number of marks were used by the factory incorporating the names of Spode and of Copeland, but far from creating confusion the mark changes are most helpful in providing accurate dating. The factory is now owned by the Royal Worcester Porcelain Company.

Worcester (and Lund's Bristol)

The story of this factory began in Bristol with the establishment there about 1748 of a soft paste porcelain manufactory owned by Benjamin Lund. It was here that Cornish soapstone was first used in a porcelain formula, known as 'soapy rock'

141

because of its slippery feel, producing the distinctive porcelain that so many collectors have come to admire. It is often impossible to separate early Lund blue-and-white and early Worcester blue-and-white. The Lund factory had a short life of some three years but the quality of production achieved in that short time was to have great influence on the subsequent success of Worcester.

Where pieces are known to be the products of the Bristol soft paste factory it is termed Lund's Bristol. The factory is believed to have been first established at Redcliffe Backs in the Bristol dock area, by someone involved in the failed London manufactory of Limehouse. The porcelain characteristics of this early Bristol include a green translucency, which is continued in the Worcester porcelain, and the glaze may be considerably blued or at times rather grey in appearance with a certain amount of sanding. There is also a tendency for the porcelain to warp and the majority of wares are moulded. As might be expected the Lund designs were largely influenced by Chinese and Japanese patterns. Marks of BRISTOL and BRISTOLL have been found on bases.

In 1752 Lund's Bristol was purchased in its entirety by the Worcester company and when the manufactory was removed to that city, some of the Bristol decorators moved with it. A partnership deed dated 4 June 1751 is in the archives of the Worcester Royal Porcelain Company, and it tells of how fourteen local men and Edmund Cave of London, the editor of *The Gentleman's Magazine*, founded the Worcester Tonquin Manufactury, later known as the Worcester Porcelain Company. Worcester remains today the only English porcelain company with an unbroken line of tradition.

It was Dr John Wall, M.D., and the apothecary William Davis who are named as having invented the Worcester formula. The years between 1751 and 1786, when Dr Wall died, are known as the Dr Wall period and, for many, it contains some of the most attractive porcelain of the eighteenth century.

A feature of the Worcester wares is the precise quality of its potting. The early decoration of Worcester is carried out in underglaze blue to be followed by Oriental overglaze in enamel. Excellent transfer printed pieces were done by Robert Hancock, and some of the finest of these are the portraits, usually found on mugs, of Frederick the Great, King of Prussia, and an ally of England in the Seven Years War.

Porcelain was also sent out of the factory for decoration, James Giles of Camden Town was a prominent decorator of this kind and was in demand by most of the leading factories. He

First standard blue crescent mark, *c.* 1755-83

Blue painted or printed mark, *c.* 1760-80

Painted 'square' or 'seal' mark in underglaze blue, *c.* 1755-75

Worcester version of the Dresden crossed-swords mark

Printed numeral marks, *c.* 1770-83

Impressed or incised marks, *c.* 1807-13

also bought porcelain in the white from factories for resale in his own retail premises in Soho after he had decorated them.

The similarity of decoration of a high standard has been noticed many times between factories and this has led to the identification of painters by style where their real names are unknown to us. Hence such descriptions as 'the cut fruit' painter, and 'the dishevelled bird' painter. Even the hand of individual painters can be identified from among the early blue-and-white porcelains. Workmen's marks appear on the wares of several factories and a large number have been recorded on Worcester pieces. More famous painters are less of a problem to identify: Fidelle Duvivier, the French-born Chelsea painter, may have worked for Worcester at the factory, and he is credited with painting Sèvres-style exotic birds on some pieces. The Irishman Jeffreys Hamet O'Neale and the Scotsman John Donaldson have signed their work for Worcester, a privilege given to very few ceramic artists in the eighteenth century.

The late Dorothy Doughty remains outstanding among a long list of superb modellers who have worked for Royal Worcester. Probably no other modeller in the history of ceramics has received such public acclaim in their own lifetime. All her models were made in limited editions, mostly between 255 and 500, after which the moulds were destroyed. Dorothy Doughty, who died in 1962, delighted in modelling birds and flowers; indeed her bird models are usually associated with flowers and plants, for this remarkable woman believed that the two were inseparable. She began by making a series of American birds of which the first pair was issued in 1935, and their success was phenomenal. Wherever possible she observed her subjects from life and the timeless quality of her work is such that she succeeded in creating a likeness close to life itself. She bequeathed three of her models to the Victoria and Albert Museum, London. All her designs of birds and flowers may also be viewed at the Dyson Perrins Museum in Worcester.

It may be useful to explain the changes in partnership that followed the death of Dr Wall, for Worcester porcelains are most often referred to by the title of the company in control at the time. Wall's successor was William Davis, who continued until his own death in 1783. The factory was then purchased by Thomas Flight, Worcester's London agent. In 1793 Martin Barr was taken into partnership, and from then on the changes in organisation became a little confusing, for example: Flight & Barr 1793-1807, Barr, Flight & Barr 1807-1813, and Flight, Barr & Barr 1813-1840.

The sale of the factory in 1783 had caused Robert Chamberlain, a decorator, to leave and set up a studio of his own in King Street, Worcester. He began by painting porcelain in the white from Caughley, and he started his own factory for porcelain manufacture in 1792 on the site of the present Worcester factory. The Chamberlain factory introduced a porcelain of quite exceptional quality in 1811 and called it 'Regent'. It was in honour of the Prince of Wales who had become Regent in that year. Perhaps the greatest commission they ever received had come a few years earlier, a service for Lord Nelson in 1802.

Standard impressed mark, c. 1813-40

144

128 *Right:* 'King of Prussia' mug. Worcester, 1757. Observe the fine potting, the reeded handle, and the superb transfer decoration based on engravings by Robert Hancock. Frederick the Great of Prussia was England's ally during the Seven Years War (1756-63).

129 *Far right:* Compote dish from the 'Shakespeare' service made by the Worcester factory of Kerr & Binns. The parian figures are of Quince and Flute from *A Midsummer Night's Dream,* and are modelled by W. B. Kirk. Dyson Perrins Museum of Worcester Porcelain, Worcester.

Standard printed or impressed mark, *c.* 1862-75

Difficult trading conditions and the fierce competition from the improved earthenware and stoneware of the Potteries caused the amalgamation of Chamberlain's factory with the original one. In 1840 Flight, Barr & Barr moved to the Chamberlain factory. From 1840 until 1851 the factory was called Chamberlain & Co., and even the Great Exhibition did little to raise the company's standing.

After the Exhibition the factory was taken over by W. G. Kerr, a partner in the Chamberlain Co., and R. W. Binns. This partnership restored Worcester porcelain to its proper place in English ceramics. From 1852 to 1862 new products appeared and new highly talented decorators emerged. In 1862 when Kerr retired, his partner formed a joint stock company and the firm became the Worcester Royal Porcelain Company.

130 An example of the remarkable 'Limoges' style of decoration perfected by Thomas Bott at the Kerr and Binns factory, 1859. The cup and saucer with its two handles is inspired by the Greek kylix shape, and is painted in white enamel on a deep blue ground. Victoria and Albert Museum, London.

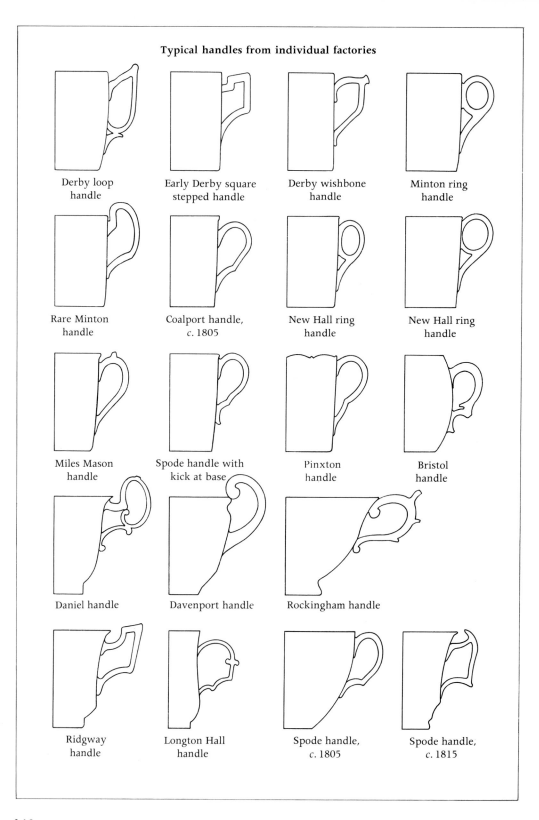

Typical handles from individual factories

Derby loop handle

Early Derby square stepped handle

Derby wishbone handle

Minton ring handle

Rare Minton handle

Coalport handle, c. 1805

New Hall ring handle

New Hall ring handle

Miles Mason handle

Spode handle with kick at base

Pinxton handle

Bristol handle

Daniel handle

Davenport handle

Rockingham handle

Ridgway handle

Longton Hall handle

Spode handle, c. 1805

Spode handle, c. 1815

Chapter 7

The nineteenth century

Whereas the eighteenth century had been one of the ceramic entrepreneurs, so the nineteenth century was quick to follow in the wake of the pioneers and their valuable discoveries, and to build upon them. Development and innovation followed one upon the other; more factories, new forms of ceramic bodies, and advances in decorative techniques. Markets were expanding rapidly, although all were to suffer in varying degrees during the 'hungry forties'. Above all, the earlier sense of adventure was maintained. There was much cross-fertilization of ideas between Britain and the Continent, and there was an increasing awareness of design. As the nineteenth century progressed so did the recognition of machine methods of production and the need to balance such advances with something of the old craft skills of hand and eye. It was such thought that led to the establishment of the art potteries whose work is now increasingly sought by collectors.

A man who bridged the two centuries well was Miles Mason (1752-1822), who described himself so accurately and delightfully as a chinaman. Born at Dent, Yorkshire, he eventually left the wool town to work for an uncle in London. He then joined Richard Farrar, a glass merchant and chinaman; later he married Farrar's daughter.

When the Napoleonic war seriously affected his trade as an importer of Oriental porcelain, he gave up the business and began the manufacture of porcelain in partnership at Liverpool and then, in the year before Trafalgar, he set up his own manufactory at Lane Delph, near Newcastle-under-Lyme. Here he produced good quality porcelain and continued doing so until 1813. Some pieces carry a tiny impressed mark, sometimes on the edge of the base, which can be difficult to find.

Mason's ironstone

For most people the mention of the name Mason means 'ironstone': it is a trade-name that indicates strength, an attribute

M. MASON

Standard impressed mark, c. 1800-13

MILES

MASON

Blue printed mark, found on willow-pattern porcelain, c. 1800-13

that should have made it commercially attractive. Ironstone was not, however, the invention of Miles Mason, but of his son Charles James Mason, who took out a patent in 1813. In the words of the patent the formula consisted of '. . . slag of ironstone, pounded and ground in water in certain proportions with flint, Cornwall stone and clay, and blue oxide of cobalt'.

Most of the patterns used to decorate the ironstone were in the Japan style and the ware was produced in large quantity. Although it was both attractive and cheap to produce, commercial success eluded ironstone and the enterprise of Charles James Mason failed. The moulds, patterns and plates were bought by Francis Morley of Shelton who had purchased the business of Hicks, Meigh and Johnson, also ironstone manufacturers. Morley gave ironstone new impetus, producing a greater variety of wares, and he turned ironstone into a flourishing business. He gained a medal at the French Exhibition of 1855, but four years later he retired and the new purchaser was the wealthy Ashworth family from Lancashire. In 1881 it was bought by the Goddards, who in 1973 sold the company to Wedgwood, who have considerably revived the output of ironstone yet again.

The Ashworths introduced a great variety into their production and ironstone became highly popular. Fine gilding, Indian patterns, floral studies, mazarine blue, relief moulded jugs, and some rare painted pieces joined the ubiquitous Imari patterns. It would have pleased Miles Mason, who had originally sought to provide a substitute for the massive imports of Chinese porcelain into England.

PATENT IRONSTONE CHINA

Impressed mark, *c.* 1813+

Standard printed mark, *c.* 1815+

131 *Left:* Three examples of Mason's work. In the foreground is a porcelain sugar box; the two dishes are both of ironstone, the one on the right being landscape-painted and rare, while that on the left bears the more common 'japan' decoration.

132 *Opposite:* Six pot lids by Felix Pratt of Fenton.

149

133 An example of the
excellent colour printing
achieved by Felix Pratt of
Fenton. Victoria and Albert
Museum, London.

134 *Right:* The 'Hop Jug', an impressive example of Victorian Majolica ware. Minton, *c.* 1860. Victoria and Albert Museum, London.

135 *Below:* Ruskin pottery with flambé glazes by William Howson Taylor.

Transfer printed wares

Transfer printed earthenware in underglaze blue also became a massive commercial success in the nineteenth century. The process was introduced by Thomas Turner at Caughley in 1780. Among the most popular designs were various forms of chinoiserie, although the most celebrated of these, the willow pattern, did not appear in its true form until 1819.

There are a few rare and early examples of hand-painted willow pattern, but these are obviously the exception. Before 1800 the transfer decoration was line engraved, but after that date stipple engravings are most common.

Thomas Minton had worked on the early Caughley plates when he was with Turner. After leaving him he engraved the pattern for other manufacturers, in each case with slight differences. It will be noticed that the number of figures on the bridge may vary, or there may be no figures at all. The pagoda

136 *Opposite:* A superb Minton pâte-sur-pâte vase, signed Marc Louis Solon.

137 *Right:* The willow pattern – perhaps the most familiar decoration on tableware. In this example, the pattern has been applied by transfer underglaze in Indian blue. Wedgwood.

may be seen in different positions, apples on the tree may vary vary in number; the fence design changes from maker to maker. Manufacturers who were swift to see the interest of the pattern were Adams, Spode, Davenport and Wedgwood, and they continued the pattern over long periods; but it should be remembered that there were nearly two hundred manufacturers of willow pattern before 1865.

The story that the willow pattern represents must surely be well known, although it is a modern one. Briefly, it is that of a Chinese mandarin who lived in a pagoda, by an apple tree, near a bridge, over which a willow tree throws its shade. The mandarin's daughter had been promised in marriage to an old but wealthy merchant, but she was secretly meeting a young man with whom she was in love. When their meetings were discovered the girl was locked in a room overlooking a river, but on the day of her marriage with the merchant she and the young man eloped. The pursuit by her father is usually shown by the figures on the bridge, the two young people having endeavoured to make their escape by boat. But when they were caught they escaped the mandarin's anger by being transformed into doves, or, as the old Staffordshire rhyme has it:

Two pigeons flying high;
Chinese vessels sailing by;
Weeping willows hanging o'er;
Bridge with three men—if not four—
Chinese temple there it stands
Seems to take up all the land;
Apple trees with apples on;
A pretty fence to end my song.

It is very difficult to attribute unmarked specimens of transfer printed earthenware in underglaze blue, although attention to detail may well identify the manufacturer. Attention to the base of the plate or dish is particularly important, noting foot-rims and of course any marks. Most of the old pieces tend to have glazes that produce a rippled effect and the colour range of the blue printing may vary from a dark, strong blue down to an extremely light blue; also look for signs of wear on bases—this can at least indicate some degree of age. Printed earthenware of this type has risen considerably in value since the 1960s; even so, fine examples of this process may still be found without too much difficulty, and in the author's view are still considerably undervalued. Although the early transfer prints are based on Chinese designs, it was not long before engravings were being made of typical English rural scenes, including country houses, castles and other celebrated landmarks and buildings. A large trade was also maintained with North America and those pieces bearing scenes of American interest are much in demand on that continent.

The success of a print, apart from meeting the interests and requirements of the general public, depended on a good engraver, an artist able to cut his design into a copper plate by means of either lines or dots. The closer the lines or dots the darker the colour became. The printing ink was usually cobalt blue, mixed with flint into an oily pigment. After first warming the copper plate, ink was spread on with a palette knife in order to work the pigment into the etched detail. The surface of the plate was then wiped clean and the transfer paper was applied, enabling it to pick up the impression which was to be transferred ink-side down on the ware to be decorated. Printed borders were applied separately and the joins can often be seen, particularly when the transfer was applied in several sections. After the paper was removed the pattern on the ware was fixed by heating in a muffle oven, which remains at a low temperature. This was followed by dipping the object in glaze which was in turn fixed in a glost oven. Such a process produced bright, attractive, hard wearing products to which so many collections now testify. Examples printed in this manner are at their best between 1800 and 1825. As well as the subjects already mentioned animal and sporting subjects also became popular, as did Italian and Indian scenes. John and William Ridgway of Caldon Place made a superb series of views of Oxford and Cambridge colleges.

Other outstanding examples came from the Spode works at Stoke-on-Trent. Spode were among the first potters to manufacture blue printed wares, and the story of Spode transfer printing is better charted than that of any other Staffordshire pottery. Of quite extraordinary interest are the early nineteenth-century services with scenes of Indian sport. It includes such titles as 'Hog Hunter Meeting by surprise a Tiger', 'Syces or Grooms leading out Horses', and 'Dooreans, or Dog Keepers leading out Dogs'. It is a series that seems to reflect Britain's continuing interest in India, but the scenes themselves were taken from a book published in London in 1805 under the title *Oriental Field Sports, Wild Sports of the East,* written by Captain Williamson, with aquatints by Thomas Howitt. Illustrated books of a sporting or topographical nature were to have increasing influence upon ceramic artists.

Pot lids

The colour-printed pot lid of the nineteenth century is something that most people easily recognise. Pot lids were the work
of F. and R. Pratt of Fenton in Staffordshire and were made
between 1846 and 1880. From 1846 to 1849 the lids were decorated in only two colours but improved mechanical processes were to change all that. The earlier pottery of the firm
known as Pratt ware has already been mentioned in Chapter 4,
but the nineteenth-century wares, decorated with polychrome
transfer prints, must not be confused with the earlier products.
Jesse Austin of Longton (1806-1879) was the major figure in
colour printing during the nineteenth century and it was he
who developed the process for decorating the pot lids. He had
much in common with George Baxter, inventor of Baxter
prints. Baxter's technique was to apply the engraving first and
subsequently use a number of other plates to apply the separate colours; it called for exact methods of working in order
to ensure the correct registration of each colour to prevent
overlap. Jesse Austin applied the same principle but the other
way about. He used up to five plates in each work, but applied
the colours first and the engraving last. Some of his pot lids are
signed, either with his name in full or with his initials. The
interest in these is very understandable for the illustrations
portray a great deal of the life, events, and topography of that
period as well as earlier historical occasions and characters.
There are a host of pod lids covering such diverse subjects as
the Australian gold strike, the Crimean war, and the plays of
Shakespeare.

During the 1840s small earthenware pots were in demand.
The new industries of fish paste and potted shrimps demanded
containers. At the same time powdered wigs were now only
occasionally to be seen and men displayed their natural hair
although heavily greased. The containers of this grease were
known as pomade pots, and frequently have bear designs – the
pomade inside was in fact bear's grease. As the highly commercial paste and pomade pots became widely popular a
number of other Staffordshire potters began to make them.
The great shrimping company Tantell and Son, used some
fifteen different designs connected with Pegwell Bay for their
product. These are among the more common pot lids.

The majority of pot lids found have rather convex surfaces,
and the earliest lids have a tendency towards unevenness but are
basically flat and smaller in diameter than the later ones. Many
reproduction pot lids have been made, but most of the early

lids show signs of crazing. If you suspended an early lid from your finger and tapped it with a pencil the resultant sound should be completely dull, whereas a reproduction may produce a ringing sound. Another point is that the old colours are invariably brilliant, particularly the reds and the blues.

Parian

During the nineteenth century outstanding works of ceramic art were achieved by the firms of Copeland and Minton respectively. Here we will deal with the discovery that first belongs to Copeland, that is the successful production of an unglazed biscuit porcelain that in appearance resembles marble; hence its name, inspired by the marble from the island of Paros. By far the majority of parian is white but some examples are tinted. While 1846 is generally regarded as the date when parian was first launched upon the world, one account declares that it was first introduced in 1842. This is contained in Hunt's *Handbook to the Official Catalogues of the Great Exhibition* published in 1851.

' The first idea of imitating marble in ceramic manufacture originated by Mr. Thomas Battan, the artist directing the extensive porcelain manufactory of Mr. Alderman Copeland at Stoke-upon-Trent, in the commencement in 1842. After a series of experiments he succeeded in producing a very perfect imitation of marble, both in surface and tint. One of the earliest specimens was submitted to His Grace the Bishop of Sutherland who expressed his unqualified admiration of the purposes to which it was applied, and became its first patron by purchasing the example submitted. This was on the 3rd August 1842 . . .'

Hunt is not regarded as a particularly reliable writer although it is obvious from reports in the Art Union magazine that Messrs Copeland and Garrett were producing fine parian wares well before 1846. The Art Union of London were intensely concerned about the relationship between mass manufacture and art, and they decided to issue a fine statue, in a limited edition, made of stone china as manufactured by Messrs Copeland and Garrett. The interest of the sculptor John Gibson, RA, proved readily forthcoming, and the first figure to be commissioned by the Art Union of London was his 'The Narcissus' in parian. Other similar societies were also important in providing a stimulus to artistic manufacture. Prince Albert was ready to give these Unions his blessing 'feeling assured that these Institutions will exercise a most beneficial influence on the Arts'. Fifty parian copies were made of 'The Narcissus' when it was completed in 1846. The copies were given as prizes and had cost the Art Union £3 each – for which sum, ten years ago, they might well have been purchased at auction. Parian figures are of outstanding quality and it can only be that their lack of colour was the reason for the twentieth-century buying public's cool attitude towards them. Once again we have the situation of quality being overlooked for a long period and the result is that the best parian figures

138 Two parian figures. In the foreground is Narcissus by John Gibson made by Copeland and the first such model to be commissioned by the Art Union of London in 1846. In the background is a Minton parian figure of a dancer.

139 'Innocence', a parian porcelain figure. Copeland, 1847. Victoria and Albert Museum, London.

are now climbing considerably in value, and are unlikely ever again to fall.

'The Narcissus' proved highly popular with the members of the Art Union, with the result that many more such figures were commissioned by them. Parian examples that were used for prizes will always be found to be marked, either printed or impressed to that effect. In some ways the Art Unions were similar to the book clubs and record clubs of the twentieth century.

The Art Union of London was established in 1836, each member paying an annual subscription entitling him to take part in an annual draw or raffle. The main prizes were all works of art, usually paintings from Royal Academy Exhibitions. It was immediately clear that the new statuary porcelain or parian was the perfect medium for filling the role of the lesser prizes. As they grew in popularity more prizes of a ceramic nature were introduced and while the Art Unions succeeded in their endeavours to raise the standard of design, they also engendered a similar awareness among their prize winners who may never otherwise have purchased the objects concerned.

Even though Copelands were undoubtedly the first to produce parian on a commercial basis, and certainly, in the production of figure groups, there are earlier claims for its invention, e.g. Thomas Boote of Burslem who claimed its manufacture in 1841, and Messrs Minton were also pioneers in the field and produced some excellent figure models.

Majolica

The word Majolica is frequently used to indicate tin glazed wares in the Italian Maiolica style, but it should really be applied only to English earthenware decorated in coloured lead glazes; in particular those of Minton for which Majolica was a trade name.

In 1850 Majolica joined the many other art products of Minton and although it became a fashionable ware of the period, and most other factories made wares of a similar type, Minton reigned supreme. It was part of the factory's policy of re-introducing many of the Renaissance styles which they did with great aplomb – but none achieved such popular success as Majolica. The vigorous character of the wares they made and the purity of colour and glaze created several minor works of art. Most remarkable among the Majolica was a life-sized model of a peacock by the French sculptor Paul Comolera from Limoges. Comolera undertook the modelling and decoration

140 *Far left:* Moulded white stoneware 'Minster' jug with figures in Gothic niches, by Charles Meigh of Hanley, *c.* 1840. Victoria and Albert Museum, London.

141 *Below:* Minton vase in the Sèvres style with rose Pompadour ground and painted panels. Minton, *c.* 1905.

142 Victorian Majolica group showing a cupid figure riding a sea-horse. Minton, 1859. Victoria and Albert Museum, London.

using hand painted soft colour glazes. After three years Comolera returned to France and only five such peacocks were made. Majolica glazed cockerels by John Henk, standing $13\frac{1}{2}$ inches (340 mm) high, are also of immense quality, but it was such satisfying wares as the covered 'hop' jug that found popular appeal on the mass market and were produced over several years.

Pâte-sur-pâte

In the second half of the nineteenth century a series of porcelains of great richness emerged from Minton. Artists and designers of international repute came from the Continent to work at Stoke-on-Trent. The reason they came was the success in international exhibitions that Minton achieved after their large scale display at the Great Exhibition of 1851.

A French influence began to pervade the Minton factory. Not only the Sèvres ground colours were copied but the Sèvres shapes too. The results were hand-decorated, richly gilded

161

vases and other porcelains so lavish that it is unlikely that any English manufactory will ever make such wares again. The painters of these pieces were Sèvres-trained artists of the calibre of Anton Boullemier. As well as realising that Minton were making some of the richest porcelains in Europe, there was also the knowledge that Minton's Art Director was a Frenchman, Léon Arnoux (1816-1902) who arrived at Minton towards the end of the 1840s. This was the man the *Art Journal* described as '. . . among the most talented and accomplished Frenchmen who ever honoured our shores and aided us in the development of our art industries'.

The Franco-Prussian War in 1870 proved an added incentive for French artists to come to England, and one in particular has become known to connoisseurs all over the world; his name was Marc Louis Solon. In fact Minton, Marc Louis Solon, and the technique known as pâte-sur-pâte (paste on paste) have become synonymous.

Solon's offer to work for Minton was accepted by Arnoux and he remained with them until his retirement in 1904. What

THE ARTHUR NEGUS GUIDE TO
ENGLISH POTTERY AND PORCELAIN

is more he was given encouragement to perfect his beloved pâte-sur-pâte. The process had evolved at Sèvres but Solon's work in England gave it an entirely new dimension.

The basic shape to be decorated in this manner was made in tinted parian ware but it was not fired. Then came the application by hand of 'slip' or liquid porcelain that was built up day by day until it reached the required thickness. It was a process that always took weeks and often months to achieve. Then the slip was cut in cameo fashion and fired. The diaphanous translucency achieved by this method is astonishing, but until the firing and the moment when the piece of pâte-sur-pâte emerged from the kiln it was never known whether the work of months would end in triumph or disaster. The most complex piece that Solon ever attempted took seven months to complete. Pâte-sur-pâte could only be tolerated if it were perfect, and this, coupled with the expense and time involved, dissuaded other factories from following suit although attempts were made.

Solon trained apprentices from 1873 and their names are Alboine Birks, Lawrence Birks, H. Hollins, T. Mellor, A. Morgan, Frederick Read, T. H. Rice, H. Saunders and C. Toft.

Of these students it was Alboine Birks who proved second only to Solon himself. Birks continued working on pâte-sur-pâte until his death in 1940. Very little signed work by the pupils mentioned above is found. The reason is that Solon disliked the idea.

Doulton of Lambeth

The Lambeth pottery has a long history which, as far as collectors are concerned, begins with the partnership of Doulton and Watts at the beginning of the nineteenth century. The main figure, however, in the rise of Doulton as a major pottery was Henry Doulton, who began his apprenticeship in 1835. Later in the century he was to receive a knighthood as one of the leading figures in the ceramic industry and one of the most respected luminaries of Victorian art. Henry Doulton was a man of great foresight who was quick to see talent wherever it lay and to give it every encouragement and practical help. The basic output of the Lambeth pottery was sanitary stonewares, drain pipes etc. In a century when cholera was still rife in England, the supply of Doulton stoneware water filters played a vital role in maintaining health when so many local water supplies were suspect. Today these water filters, either the large domestic model or the smaller versions for use at table, are

Vase shapes

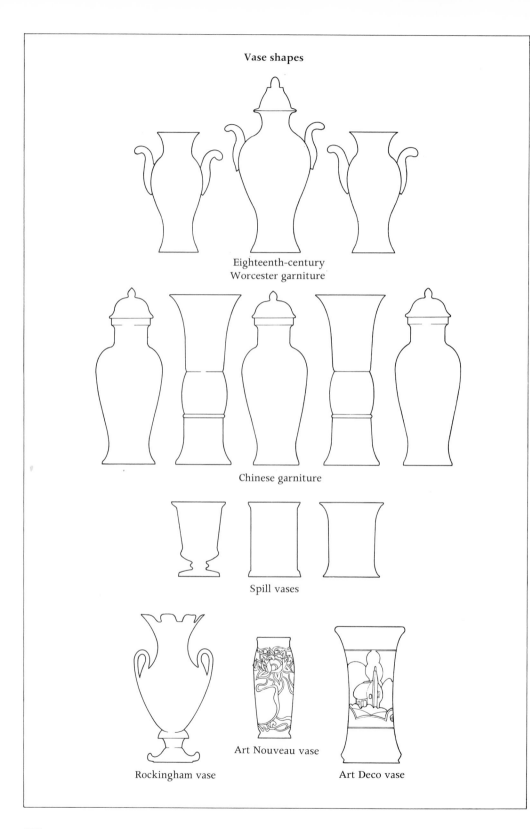

Eighteenth-century
Worcester garniture

Chinese garniture

Spill vases

Rockingham vase

Art Nouveau vase

Art Deco vase

144 Nineteenth-century Doulton stoneware vessels decorated by Hannah Barlow.

Impressed mark, *c.* 1877-80

Impressed or printed mark, *c.* 1872 +

Standard impressed mark, *c.* 1902-22 and *c.* 1927-36

Standard impressed mark, *c.* 1922-56

often collected as 'by-gones' or to provide a decorative feature in a room.

At the 1862 Exhibition, Doulton exhibited wares with simple incised designs. They were far from satisfactory but it was to sow the seed of Doulton art pottery and it soon began to flourish under Henry Doulton's enthusiastic guidance.

The Doulton decorated stonewares manufactured over the following thirty years provide a rich field for the collector. Part of Henry Doulton's philosophy of encouragement was that his artists should be permitted to sign their work; this is of course particularly attractive to the collector for such full documentary information is rarely available to him. The signatures take the form of initials or monograms incised into the clay. While the identification of such pieces is therefore a comparatively simple matter in comparison with the experience required to identify eighteenth-century unmarked wares, the artists themselves are nonetheless entirely worthy of attention and high regard.

The most celebrated decorative artists at Doulton are undoubtedly the Barlow family, in particular Hannah B. Barlow (working 1872-1906), Florence Barlow (working 1873-1909), and Arthur Barlow (died in 1879).

Hannah Barlow, like so many other of the artists of her day, created her designs with incised outlines into which colour was applied and burnt in. The proper name for this type of decoration is called *sgraffito.* Her work is unique in that none of her pieces are alike. In particular her designs depict animals, ranging from lions and horses to less exotic but equally beautiful cows.

Florence Barlow's work was similar to that of her sister but again no two pieces are alike. Her principal decoration was birds, usually raised in low relief. Arthur Barlow was the brother of Hannah and Florence, and his work differs from theirs in that he concentrated his efforts upon foliage rather than animal life. He worked at Doultons for only eight years, therefore his work is rare.

Another artist whose work has attracted collectors for many years is George Tinworth (working 1866-1913). Much of it is in the form of miniature sculpture, he produced plaques and models of children and small animals. This, however, was only part of Tinworth's career. John Ruskin regarded him as an artist of the utmost importance and encouraged him in the production of large terracotta sculpted panels. In 1883 a massive exhibition of his work was held in London, and a book superbly illustrated in photogravure, *The Critical Essay of the Life and Works of George Tinworth*, appeared the same year. Unfortunately most of the edition was destroyed in a fire at the Fine Arts Society, and this book is now of great rarity.

Eliza Simmance was also a highly productive artist who, like Arthur Barlow, was intensely interested in foliage decoration. Collectors of Art Nouveau find her particularly interesting because of the influence of the movement in her designs, some of which were by Charles Rennie Mackintosh.

The Doulton collector will find a host of other artists well worth collecting and in this respect further research is recommended.

In the early years of the Barlows' work there were no studios for them in the pottery and they worked in the Lambeth showroom at a table, with a screen between them and the public. Hannah Barlow has recorded how the artists looked forward to the daily visits of Henry Doulton, which were always courteous, enthusiastic and encouraging. She later wrote:

'When first I came to the Potteries, few people knew what reverses I had in my home, and what a dreadful undertaking it was to me to meet strangers. I shall never forget the first time I encountered Sir Henry Doulton, how great my alarm was, and how kindly and considerately he received me. He was always encouraging. He made it impossible for me not to enjoy my work, and his great love of animals made his visits to my studio most helpful. He would rarely come without telling me of some trait of the life of horses or cattle which he had observed, or some grouping of them in the fields which he believed would aid my imagination.

Artists' marks

Hannak Barlow, *c.* 1872-1906

George Tinworth, *c.* 1867-1913

Florence Barlow, *c.* 1873-1909

Arthur Barlow, *c.* 1872-79

166

'I always noticed that Sir Henry Doulton never forgot a promise . . . In all the years I have worked at Lambeth, I never once had the sensation that money was the ultimate object of my art. Sir Henry and his family have always shown an extraordinary tact in preventing such a feeling. I hold this to have been one of the great charms of my work at Lambeth. Sir Henry always seemed to urge me to do my best, without respect to its commercial value to him, and his enthusiastic interest in my designs had the effect of constantly rousing me to try to do still better things.

'Of late years, it was not possible for him to be such a constant visitor to the Studios. Since he has ceased to come, we have missed him very much. My sister Florence agrees with me that some of the pleasantest memories of our life are of the days when we began the decoration work upon the stoneware, and with them the eager and generous sympathy of Sir Henry Doulton is indissolubly connected.'

The following extracts from the writings of Sir Henry Doulton will give some insight into his attitude to his art. 'The progress of the art of pottery affords many striking instances of the laws of growth, perfection and decay. As schools of philosophy, poetry and painting are subject to rise, culmination, decay and fall, so is the potter's art. Except in the East, where tradition operates so powerfully, and where tribes, castes and families carry on their trade for ages, these industries rarely maintain their highest development through more than two or three generations.

'In our own country we have several examples of schools of pottery which have existed but are now extinct. Chelsea, Bow, Lowestoft, Liverpool, Bristol and Swansea have all become names of the past, notwithstanding their high excellence and the extensive patronage which they once received. Most of these have succumbed before the introduction of cheaper methods of decoration and more economical modes of manufacture. Indeed, it is a striking fact that, with scarcely an exception, only those potteries have been able to maintain a long-lived career which have relied for their staple manufacture on utilitarian rather than decorative wares. This principle is true even of artistic pottery. A proportion of the useful seems to be an essential condition of any degree of permanence. A school of decorative pottery only is short-lived – firstly, because it is dependent on individual taste and culture and, secondly, because it is not by itself remunerative.

'Wedgwood, Worcester and Minton have, undoubtedly,

maintained their continuous production through so long a
period by careful attention to domestic requirements as well
as original art wares.'

'There is with the public of the present time a morbid
craving after novelties, irrespective of their intrinsic
excellence, which leaves neither designer nor manufacturer
time to develop full capabilities of his productions before the
passing day of their public appreciation has gone by.
  'Of course, public taste cannot altogether be disregarded;
and if a master is to provide for the dependent army of
workers the demand must to some extent regulate the supply –
although the intelligent and enterprising manufacturer
will always endeavour to lead the public taste; certainly,
if he leaves it at too great a distance it is at a great cost.
  'It is needful that beauty of design should go hand in hand
with economy of technique; it is still more necessary that
those who have this matter in hand should realise that their
true mission is not accomplished until they have rendered art
"a language understanded of the people".
  'Then, and then only, will designers find ready outlet for
their conceptions; then and then only, will manufacturers
realise that their interest is to produce good art rather than
bad, and strive after excellence rather than novelty, after
grave rather than cheapness.'

'The artists of England cannot all be Royal Academicians of
the great luminary in Picaddilly [sic]! Some may also be

145 Ruskin pottery vase,
1922 (left), and a Martin
brothers jug decorated with
grotesques.

altogether outside the planetary system which it can weigh or measure. Yet it is possible that these neglected lights may be radiances of another and even larger system only discoverable by powers more catholic, comprehensive and accurate than Burlington House commands.'

Martin Ware

R W Martin -84
Fulham

c. 1873-74

R W Martin 9
London

c. 1874-78

R W Martin 21
Southall

OR R W MARTIN
SOUTHALL.

c. 1878

R W Martin
London & Southall

c. 1879-82

R W Martin & Brothers
London & Southall

1882+

This is the name given to the remarkable stonewares made by the Martin brothers at Fulham and at Southall between 1873 and the First World War. The idea of the individual craftsman as opposed to the mass produced item had already begun to emerge at Doultons of Lambeth, but the Martin brothers are generally regarded as being the first craftsman potters of the modern school. The four brothers are as follows:
Robert Wallace Martin (1843-1923)
Charles Douglas Martin (1846-1910)
Walter Frazer Martin (1859-1912)
Edwin Bruce Martin (1860-1915)
Edwin Martin had once worked at Doultons, where he learned the art of incising pottery. Charles carried out some decoration but mainly dealt with administration. Walter dealt with clays, glazes and firing, while Wallace was the main sculpture and modeller.

Their work is astonishing in its diversity and in the range of models and decorations described as grotesques. Although their products today are much collected and therefore valuable, they were never so prosperous during their own lifetime.

Their work is normally stamped or incised with signature marks, date and address, e.g.:
R. W. Martin. Fulham 1873-1874.
R. W. Martin, London 1874-1878.
Signature marks with address Southall 1878-1879.
Signature marks with the address London and Southall date from 1879.

'Brothers' or 'Bros' was added to the signature mark in 1882, although it will be found that most examples include the incised date of manufacture.

One of the most interesting accounts of the work involved during the firing of a kiln is to be found in the *Pall Mall Gazette* of January 1890, which contains a description of a visit made to the Martin brothers at their Southall Pottery:
'Their kiln, which stands about a hundred yards from the Grand Junction Canal, is built within an irregular-looking building of stone, cement, brick, iron and wood; the shaft,

which juts out from the centre of the roof for several feet, and the vaporous smoke, which rolls away before the wind to join the scudding clouds, being the only outward and visible signs of its inward fiery presence. On the threshold I met Mr. R. W. Martin, who at once led the way into the kiln. The heat was so terrific that the atmosphere appeared to be glassy and wavy. Two men stripped to the shirt, and with bared arms and throats, were leaning against the wall, the one resting on a long iron rod and the other on a coalheaver's shovel. They were grimed with smoke, and dust and clay, perspiration trickled down their arms and faces like rain on the panes of a window, black beads of perspiration clung to their swarthy throats, their hair was matted and their voices were as the voices of men in the Sahara Desert. The elder of the two, who had entire charge of the kiln, was Walter Martin and the younger, who was assisting him, was his brother Edwin. They had both been at work in that building, turn and turn about, since Thursday midday, and for the last twenty hours Edwin Martin had never left the fires. "How can you stand this fearful heat?" I asked. They said that it was "nothing", and Walter Martin, after having cautioned me to "stand by", opened the door of one of the fires directly opposite to where I was standing, and said, "Now that *is* heat". It was indeed: he closed the door again in an instant, but not before I felt as though I had been done through and through. Then they began to coal up for the last time before salting off. Each of the five doors at the base of the kiln was opened in quick succession and large logs of wood and shovels of coal thrown in to feed the fire. Each time a door was opened the heat became well-nigh unbearable—the wooden beams and rafters became so hot that I could scarcely bear to touch them, and iron girders and binders warped like warm sealing-wax. Next they mounted a narrow flight of stairs leading to the floor above, from whence they stoked the kiln in five more places, but there the heat was not so fierce. At the base of the kiln it was impossible to get more than about four feet distant from the fires; neither was it possible to stand upright, because the beams and rafters of the floor above were not more than about five feet from the ground, while upstairs there was plenty of breathing space. As Walter Martin went from firehole to firehole I noticed that he limped painfully; an iron lean-to had fallen overnight, he told me, and struck his foot a crushing blow, and what with the heat and the continual exertion it had gradually become extremely painful. As time wore on the heat grew more intense. The beams and rafters scorched and blackened and had to be drenched with salt and water to prevent them from bursting into flames. I looked into the kiln from above, while the salt was being put in to glaze the pottery, and saw the raging fury of the flames in all their gorgeous splendour . . . And there, within that living hell, splendid examples of the potter's skill were being fired without protection of any kind. While others protect their wares with "saggers" or "slugs" these potters are content to trust theirs to the most terrible of the elements in *puris naturalibus.* How they can have the courage to run the risk is almost inconceivable. Meantime Walter Martin's foot became worse, and he had to be provided with a stick to lean on while he worked with his right hand; and, finally, a pair of crutches were procured for him from a neighbouring cottage. He grew anxious. He had packed the kiln, and only he could fire it off. If an accident happened, or if an error of judgment were committed, four months' work might, and probably would, be either destroyed or rendered valueless. But he stuck to his post like a man, and, although occasionally he groaned aloud with agony, he resolutely went round and round the fires, up stairs and down again, shovelled the salt in, tried his proofs, had the fires once more renewed and superintended the plugging of the fireholes to exclude the draught. Then, his labours having for the time being come to an end – for it takes five days for the kiln to cool – he was carried by his brothers in to the cottage, his foot was dressed, and he was wheeled home on a tricycle to sleep the sleep of the brave and the just.'

Other art potters and potteries whose work will repay further study and will no doubt be increasingly collected in future years, are as follows:

William De Morgan, born 1836. After early experiments in tile decoration he set up a kiln in Cheyne Walk, Chelsea, between 1872 and 1881. From 1882 to 1888 he worked at a kiln at Merton Abbey, Wimbledon, moving to Fulham in 1888. Among his partners were the artists Charles and Fred Passenger.

The Compton Pottery, Guildford. Started by Mary Watts, wife of the celebrated Victorian painter. The pottery closed in 1956.

The Della Robbia Pottery, Birkenhead, began in 1894 and produced some fine vases decorated in enamels and coloured glazes.

146 'Tree of Life' bowl by Bernard Leach, c. 1923. Victoria and Albert Museum, London.

The Watcombe Pottery, south Devon, established in 1869. Wide range of products including terracottas.

William Moorcroft of Burslem, Staffordshire. Moorcroft began his design career in 1897 and died in 1945. Produced a wide range of shapes and decoration, and has particularly come into prominence during the last ten years.

Pilkington's Lancastrian Pottery, near Manchester. Established 1891.

Ruskin Pottery, Smethwick, established by W. Howson-Taylor in 1898. The pottery takes its name from Howson-Taylor's regard for Ruskin. Just before his death in 1935 he destroyed all his materials and papers, and wrote in a letter to a friend: 'Why let another firm make rubbish and call it Ruskin?'

Clarice Cliff. This remarkable lady designed for the industrial factory rather than the small studio concern. Her designs bear her facsimile signature. While intense interest is now being given to her work the author believes that the collector should concentrate upon acquiring major examples of her designs.

Charles Vyse. Charles Vyse and his wife, had, like William De Morgan, a kiln at Cheyne Walk, Chelsea. He was responsible for some very interesting figure groups that were decorated by his wife. Their studio was established in 1919.

There are a large number of art potteries to be considered by the collector and there is an increasingly large amount of information and literature published on the subject. The doyen of English art potters is Bernard Leach, who was born in 1887. His knowledge and understanding of Oriental pottery and his intensive studies under Japanese master potters has greatly influenced not only his own work, but also the work of other distinguished potters and countless aspiring students.

Glossary

Acid gilding Method of gilding using acid to create a pattern on the body of an article, leaving areas untouched by it in relief. The surface is then gilded and the parts untouched by acid are polished with an agate, leaving the remainder matt.

Applied flowers Term used when flowers are modelled or moulded separately before being affixed to a vase or figure.

Ball clay Pipe-clay from Dorset and Devon so called because it was originally transported to the potters in large balls.

Basalt A black, hard unglazed body able to take a polish, introduced by Wedgwood in the 1760s.

Bat printing A design first created on a copper plate but transferred to the object being decorated by a 'bat' or slab of gelatine. The result is more delicate than the usual line engraving.

Biscuit Term used for objects of unglazed and undecorated porcelain after the first firing.

Body (paste) Material or materials that form the basic substance of any ceramic object.

Bone ash Ox-bones reduced to ash, today usually obtained from the Argentine and India.

Café-au-lait A soft brown, used either as a ground colour or plain, banded or decorated.

Ceramics Name given to all types of fired clays, whether pottery or porcelain.

Chinoiserie European version of an Oriental scene or style.

Cottages Name given to the many models of cottages and houses made in Staffordshire as pastille burners.

Crazing The minute mesh or tracing of lines that appears in the glaze of some factories' products e.g. eighteenth-century Derby.

Delft Soft clay body with a hard opaque white tin glaze.

Famille jaune Term used to describe a whole range of yellow enamels. It is particularly used as a ground colour, often with decoration from the green palette.

Famille noire A so-called black enamel used by the Chinese. It is decorated from the green palette.

Famille rose A beautiful pink enamel first made in Europe and introduced into China during the late seventeenth century. The Chinese developed it and used it extensively, particularly on their export wares.

Famille verte Green enamel, among the earliest of enamels used by the Chinese.

Foot-rim The turned foot upon which most plates, cups and dishes stand.

Glost kiln Kiln in which objects receive their second firing in order to mature the glaze.

Hollow ware Literally, items that are hollow, such as cups, bowls and teapots, in contrast to flatware like plates and dishes.

Ironstone Strong, heavy earthenware patented by Charles Mason in 1813.

Lithophane Thin porcelain plaques with an intaglio moulded decoration that shows up best when viewed under strong light. Originally made on the Continent, they were produced in England during the nineteenth century, but marked specimens are rare.

Mocha ware Banded mugs and jugs with a curious tree-like decoration. These often bear an excise mark, as many of them were used in taverns.

Pot bank Very early, primitive form of kiln, used by individual potters. The name remained in use long after the introduction of more sophisticated technology in eighteenth-century industrial potteries.

Sagger Container in which ware is fired in the kiln.

Sang de boeuf The term used for the ox-blood glaze used for its brilliant and lustrous effects.

Slip Finely ground clay mixed with water for glazing or decorating earthenware.

Soufflé Name given to an attractive powder blue ground. The colour was used under the glaze and was applied in powder form, the decorator blowing it onto the porcelain through a bamboo tube. In English porcelain the term *soufflé* is substituted for 'powder blue' which does not indicate the shade of blue used but the method of applying it.

Throwing The process of actually forming pots on a potter's wheel.

Tyg Drinking vessel with several handles.

Bibliography

Jewitt's Ceramic Art Of Great Britain 1800-1900, revised by G. A. Godden, Barrie & Jenkins, 1972.

English Pottery And Porcelain, W. B. Honey, A. & C. Black, 1962.

Wedgwood Ware, A. Kelly, Ward Lock, 1970.

English Delftware, F. H. Garner, Faber & Faber, 1972.

Royal Doulton 1815-1965, D. Eycles, Hutchinson, 1965.

Spode, A History Of The Family Factory And Wares From 1733-1833, L. Whiter, Barrie & Jenkins, 1970.

Blue And White Transfer Ware, 1780-1840, A. W. Coysh, David and Charles, 1970.

English Blue And White Porcelain, B. Watney, Faber & Faber, 1963.

The Handbook Of British Pottery And Porcelain Marks, G. M. Godden, Herbert Jenkins, 1968.

British Porcelain, An Illustrated Guide, G. A. Godden, Barrie & Jenkins, 1974.

British Pottery, An Illustrated Guide, G. A. Godden, Barrie & Jenkins, 1974.

USEFUL ADDRESSES

Wedgwood:

Josiah Wedgwood and Sons Limited, Barlaston, Stoke-on-Trent, ST12 9ES

The factory has a special 'Visitor Centre', with a museum and a demonstration hall where the traditional manufacturing processes can be seen. At the museum the Assistant Curator will answer queries and supply a guide to the various year-marks (indicating year of manufacture) on nineteenth-century Wedgwood pieces.

Worcester:

Worcester Royal Porcelain Company, Merrivale House, Deansway, Worcester, WR1 2JH

The Group Public Relations Officer will supply a guide to the year-marks on nineteenth-century Worcester items, as well as more general information. The *Dyson Perrins Museum* (Severn Street, Worcester) has the finest collection of Worcester in England and will also supply information on the history of the firm and its wares, on the composition of the porcelain, and on marks.

Spode:

Spode Limited, Stoke-on-Trent, ST4 1BX

The Historical Adviser will give information on the history of the firm and its wares, and will supply a guide to marks. It is also possible to tour the factory by special arrangement.

Royal Crown Derby, Doulton and Minton:

Royal Doulton Tablewares Limited, PO Box 100, London Road, Stoke-on-Trent, ST4 7QD

It is possible to visit each of these three factories now owned by Royal Doulton. Royal Crown Derby and Minton have museums, and monthly open days for the public to bring in pieces to be identified. A Doulton museum is due to open in the near future. The Historical Adviser for the Doulton Group will send booklets on the background and development of the factories, as well as on marks and other details of identification.

The *Gladstone Pottery Museum, Longton, Staffordshire* is an industrial museum in the form of a nineteenth-century Pottery where the original kilns and methods of production can still be seen.

Index